MEMOIRS

of a

DRAG QUEEN

La Princess

February 2008
Copyright Pending
ISBN 978-1-4276-2928-9

Acknowledgments

My deepest gratitude and admiration to *Mrs. Beck Lerewu* for assistance in writing and editing notes and assorted documents chronicling my life journey. You spent endless hours prodding me and extracting every scrap and detail of my life. At times I was so exhausted I wanted to pass out, but you helped me see it through. And my social worker, *Mary Adams*, who introduced me to her best friend Becky; my hat goes off to you. You were instrumental in keeping me on track in dealing with my psychological issues. You came to my life at just the right time, and helped me through some very difficult problems and for that I can not thank you enough. This book is dedicated to Mary Adams and those who suffer contend with Manic-Depression and loneliness.

To my hero, my champion and beloved friend, *Marie Nealson*, owner of Marie's Café. You have proven time and time again not only to be great friend and inspiration, not only to me, but to every person around you. Like myself, you are a workaholic, as well, you are truly dedicated to your three children and many grandchildren. Marie I commend you.

Many thanks to *Van, my editor*. Your tireless work to turn a complex life of ambiguity in to a piece of fine literature, and to give this book meaning and purpose I greatly appreciate. Van, you have my deepest respect and gratitude.

To *Jimenez*, Patricia Hearst female guard. Thank you for the suggestion that I disclose my involvement with the SLA (*Symbionese Liberation Army*). Your suggestion fueled my desire to write this book, and your motivation compelled me to fulfill a dream! Thank you Jimenez, wherever you are.

I would not be here today if not for my beloved *Aunt Bette*. She often asked; "When will you be finished writing that book?" To which I would reply; "Soon." I am truly sorry she did not live to witness the accomplishment. God Bless you Aunt Bette. You were and still are a great lady in my life.

To My second cousin, *La Nedra Henderson*, an amazing English teacher who asked if she could proof-read my final draft (Which I gladly accepted). There are no words to thank you for your time and dedication.

To great friends of twelve years, *Jema and her husband Jim*. Jema, you are far more than my housekeeper, you are well educated and very compassionate, and I consider you my best friend and inspiration. Your loyalty and dependability enabled me to finish writing this book. Thank you.

To my beloved mentor, former employer, and dear friend, *V.J. and Margie Ninteman*, a special mention of gratitude You not only supported me mentally, but financially. Indeed I owe you my sincere thanks and endless appreciation. A million thanks to both of you for your endless support and understanding.

And, to all my other friends who encouraged me to complete this project. To *Joseph, Eddie, Al Bisara, Jess san Roque, Sir Dirrick, Sharon, Robin Green, Silvia, John Mulrenin*, and a host of others. A millions of thanks, hugs and kisses to you all.

PROLOGUE

I was born David R. Brown in the year 1941, in the small southern town of Wiggins, Mississippi. I was sexually assaulted by not only one, but two stepfathers starting at age of five, and continuing until I was thirteen years old.

In 1955, I was sent to California to live with my Aunt Bette after being arrested, accused and charged with sexual assault for being in a mutual relationship with an eleven-year-old white boy. In the Deep South black and white relationships 'were' taboo. I stayed with Aunt Bette until such time I had to return to Mississippi, to face the charges against me.

Homeless at the age of sixteen. I faced many obstacles, heartaches and loneliness, which led to several suicide attempts. I made it through, I became a better person in the process, and developed a greater understanding of humanity.

For nearly three decades, I spent my time being shuttled between jail cells and detention homes in San Diego. I was brought in repeatedly on charges of prostitution, drugs, rape, assault with a deadly weapon, immoral acts, and even kidnapping.

In 1981 I was released from prison. I have not been in a prison since. From my experience came Princess Charmagne and this is our true life story. The story of David R. Brown, a homosexual, a masquerader, a drag queen.

MEMOIRS OF A DRAG QUEEN

MEMOIRS OF A DRAG QUEEN

A whore. A prostitute. A drag queen. What appears to be a woman, is in reality a man. Feminine, charming and pretty. Dressed in a black silk cocktail dress, flesh colored stockings, patent leather heels and sporting a black and white in-born calf fur jacket. A plain face endowed with its most valuable asset, large hazel eyes, framed by dark curly lashes and a pair of full sensual lips. A face crowned by a honey-blonde wig with golden ringlets that fell down along his slender neck, encircled by a gold inlay necklace from the Ivory Coast of Africa.

I possessed all the essence of a woman and a desire to be a woman. It was more than a psychological identity problem, it was and still is, a natural desire to pacify the feminine part of my personality.

I, David R. Brown, better known as Princess Charmagne, The Lady with Champagne taste, became a whore, a prostitute, and a drag queen at the age of seventeen. Fleeing from a broken home filled with bitter memories of the past, and from the lecherous arms of a degenerate and perverted stepfather, I went naked into the world.

I roamed the ghetto streets of San Diego day after day, sleeping in parked cars and old vacant houses by night, stealing food from grocery and drug stores by day. I kept telling myself that I couldn't go on this way. I must find some way to make a living. I became tired of stealing and sleeping in parked cars and old houses. I wanted to be somebody, to have something, but most of all, I wanted to love and be loved.

I started hanging out in the downtown area, around nightclubs and bars, the sleazier the better. The little sleep I had was in all night coffee shops, restaurants and bus stations. My youth, looks and feminine mannerisms began to catch the eyes of dirty old men, sex starved military men, and everyday common perverts. Within a short time after arriving downtown, I found myself sleeping with all sorts of men from every walk of life. It was evident that they found it sexually rewarding to make love to a young and innocent seventeen-year-old boy. One night I'd be in an exclusive hotel with an affluent elderly guy, the next night in a two-bit motel with a lovesick sailor. Whatever the situation or the occasion, I was always rewarded financially for my time and the pleasure which I afforded them. The pleasures that I received from these experiences gave me satisfaction beyond my wildest dreams. It was no surprise that I plunged even further into an emotional state of sexual confusion.

The gay world. A world of visual perception of moving objects that has no more reality than if one were watching television. A world filled with false hopes and deferred dreams. A world of boy-queens, girl-queens, pimps, whores, hustlers and prostitutes. A world where the sound of a baby crying is rare, and the signs of death are everywhere.

This was my world and I became one of its most loyal advocates. It gave me a new perspective and meaning in life that I had never known or experienced, in this world of perversion I was somebody. I was a well-known drag queen and female impersonator. Even though it was based in fantasy, for the first time in my life I was beginning to understand the meaning of love and enjoy the pleasures it provided. Whatever it gave, it was far more than the world in which I had escaped, and where I had no intentions of going back.

My fame was a combination of reality and myth. It was a blend of fact and fiction and the blonde wig I wore. Many referred to me as "The Ebony Bridget Bardot from Savannah Georgia." During one of my escapades, a struggle ensued between a police officer and me when he tried to arrest me. My wig fell off in the middle of the street on Fifth Avenue in downtown San Diego. I was so famous that there were rumors about me. One was that while fighting with the police officer, I fell in the street, and an oncoming car ran over me and severed my head. Another version was that I had been murdered by a date and he had taken my wig off, and thrown it into the street as a warning to other prostitutes.

When I was released several days later, I was surprised to find out how many people really believed those rumors. I realized then what being famous meant -- one would believe anything that was said about you, whether it was true or false. That was the price one paid to be "somebody."

My sexual experience during this stage of my life was not limited to the members of my own sex, but extended to the opposite sex as well. I often found myself in bed with a prostitute or a whore, who seemed not to get enough pleasure from the other tricks they dated. My life reached another turning point when I met my first love of the opposite sex.

She was lovely, sweet, happy and gay. She was all of those things and many more. She was my lover, friend and companion. Liz was only seventeen and I was eighteen when we first met at a party. A fem lesbian. A redheaded, green-eyed nymph. She was the unfulfilled dream of every red-blooded American boy. Another lesbian, a very close friend of mine, introduced her to me. Later, during the party I was told that Liz had first seen me walking down Broadway, not realizing that I was a drag queen. She had been captivated by my looks, and asked my friend if she knew me. Fortunately, she did, the time Liz and I spent together were the most beautiful moments of my life.

In the early 1960s, San Diego began to come alive. New construction and industry gave San Diego a new lease on life. More people began to come to town seeking employment. This meant more money, and more money meant more opportunity. The once obscure, conservative navy town got a facelift, and over time became one of the fastest growing cities in the West. During this period I prospered, and my growing popularity with the military men made me the highest paid prostitute in town.

The improvement in my financial status took me into another world. This was a world of middle and upper class homosexuals: businessmen, attorneys, city officials, local politicians, doctors, clergymen, police officers and secretaries. These were the affluent, undercover closet queens of the elite circle of the gay world. My passport into this elite class of perverts and misfits was my popularity and fame.

One evening I received a call from June, a very dear friend of mine. She said that she had been asked to invite me to a party which was to be given at a private club in Del Mar by some very private and exclusive members of the elite gays in San Diego. June told me that, since they had heard so much about me, they wanted to meet me and learn more about my life as a well-known drag queen.

I was also curious about their lifestyle and how they felt about hiding their sexual preference from the all-seeing eyes of society. I accepted the invitation with one stipulation -- I insisted that I be allowed to come dressed anyway I chose. The request was granted.

The club was set in the western hills, just off Interstate 5, northwest of San Diego and surrounded by lush green trees and California summer landscape. The club was packed. I wondered if it was because of me or if it was just the typical weekend crowd. My question was answered when, immediately upon my arrival, I became the center of attention. I was introduced to one person after another, chatting here and there.

I saw it all. There were lesbians dressed in conservative styled ladies business suits, slacks and French-cuffed shirts. Men were dressed in fashionable three-piece suits with ties, casual slacks, shirts, and Eisenhower coats. The scene could have easily been in a Washington, D.C. club patronized exclusively by politicians and diplomats. I drank, danced and talked. When it was all over the whole crowd was convinced that I indeed was *the* Princess, and only Princess, of San Diego. After an 'after-hours' get-together at a noted county surgeon's home in Mission Hills, I returned back to the naked reality of Fifth Avenue and to the flashing neon signs that welcomed me home.

Halloween is a very special occasion throughout the Gay World. This is the one night when it is completely "legal" to dress any way one chooses. According to city ordinance, dragging was illegal, but on Halloween night it was permissible. The Halloween of 1960 was an unforgettable night. I was at my apartment getting ready to attend the annual Queens' Ball at the Elks Club in the heart of the black ghetto. I had just finished applying the final touches to my makeup when the doorbell rang. I opened the door quickly expecting the taxi I had called earlier. Instead a uniformed chauffeur was standing at attention and smiling.

He asked me if I was Princess Charmagne. I hesitated briefly and replied, "I am Princess Charmagne." "Well," he said, "I've been hired by someone who wishes to remain anonymous. I will be your personal chauffeur for the next forty-eight hours." I was stunned and amazingly curious about who this secret person could be, and what possessed him to spend a small fortune to have me chauffeured around town. There was no point wasting time in speculating on the why and how of the situation. "Just go with it and enjoy it," I told myself. I finished dressing and was escorted to the waiting black, shiny limousine by the ever-smiling chauffeur.

When the long black limousine pulled to a stop in front of the Elks Club, people began to gather in a crowd around the car. The chauffeur got out and came around the side of the car and opened the back door. I slowly appeared from the dark luxurious leather seat into the gaping crowd of curious bystanders. I stood on the sidewalk for a moment while the chauffeur secured the limousine. I heard the whispers "It's Charmagne, It is La Princess, My! How beautiful she is, She must have struck it big." The scene was magnetic and I felt a sense of power floating through my blood as I marveled at the effect that the appearance of wealth has on people.

I was wearing an elegant black evening gown that was cut especially for my slender boyish figure. The green emerald stones around my neck enhanced my feminine qualities and complimented the blonde wig that flowed gracefully and freely down the sides of my face. All my expensive attire, personal charm and physical beauty, was not enough to win the coveted award of the evening, the title of Miss San Diego of 1960. It would be three more years before I would be honored as Miss San Diego, Queen of the Halloween Ball.

After the ball, I cruised around town enjoying the attention I was receiving as the limousine made its way up and down the avenues and streets of downtown San Diego. As we passed the plaza in the center of downtown, I noticed a very handsome sailor dressed in whites standing at the bus stop on Fourth Avenue. He looked like a stranger to the world around him. I could tell he was naive to the happenings of city life, and that he was alone and a long way from home. I asked the chauffeur to pull to the curb where he was standing, and I asked the sailor if he needed a ride. His smooth ebony face contrasting the whiteness of his uniform showed a mixture of surprise and curiosity. Before he could answer I added, "What's the matter sailor boy? Are you afraid of little old me?" He smiled and said, "Of course not." I opened the door and he got into the back seat beside me. We took off down Fourth Avenue toward Market Street. Before we reached my apartment on Sixteenth and L Street, he told me a great deal about himself and I told him many things about myself. Name: Eugene Davis; Age: 19; born in Cleveland, Ohio and had been in the Navy only six months. This was the first time he had been away from home, and tonight would be his first experience into the forbidden world of homosexuality.

For the rest of the night, the nakedness of two souls dancing together in the ritual of a forbidden love reflected in thousands of mirrors that graced the walls and ceiling of the bedroom. The next morning we went shopping and had lunch at a seafood restaurant on nearby Coronado Island. When the limousine pulled to a stop in front of my apartment late that afternoon, we looked like two teenagers, just married and coming home to our new apartment.

There was no need for formalities. We understood each other. When he left the next morning to go back to the base, I knew for sure he would return that night. This would be the first time that I ever shared my life so intimately with another man. Whether our love was morally wrong or not didn't matter to us, we enjoyed a happiness that only two people in love could afford. But, like all things in life, the road must end someday and somehow, and we were no exception to this universal rule.

CHAPTER ONE

As a little black boy growing up in a small southern town in the heart of Mississippi I knew I was different from all the other children around me. I wore a steel brace on my left leg to walk. My mother told me I was born with polio. The doctor said I would never walk straight without braces.

My medical problems loomed large in my life, and there were other things that contributed to my feelings of insecurity. My large hazel eyes framed by dark curly lashes and other feminine attributes made me the target of teasing by all my classmates. Was it reality or just my insecurities?

During class I would often sit by myself, at recess I would go alone into the fields near the school to listen to the birds sing and watch the beautiful butterflies. Snakes would become my friends. They filled the loneliness I felt as a result of being shunned by my peers and rejected by my own family. I began to create a world of illusion with my newfound friends. They filled the emptiness within me because with them there was no need to hide my feelings and pretend not to be different. They accepted me as I was. These creatures did not tease or call me names as did my peers. It was the teasing and name calling that my depression and caused me to entertain thoughts of suicide. My new world seemed to provide me with a certain amount of peace and security, but the reality of my being was still visible and the pain it caused still lingered deep in my soul.

The mere thought of wearing braces for the rest of my life was devastating to me. I saw other kids with polio wearing braces. They seemed awkward, clumsy and lonely to me. I was determined to overcome this obstacle no matter what it took to achieve this goal.

I was determined to walk and no one was going to stop me. My Aunt Bette would take me to the doctor every week. She had faith and she finally convinced the doctor that someday I would walk without the brace on my left foot. Her faith proved to be my salvation. When I was about three years old, at the beginning of World War II, I was crossing the street not far from home and a big Army truck almost ran over me. God was watching over me that day. Since then he has continued to watch over me and bless me with his goodness and kindness. Today I walk with no sign of ever having had polio and no sign of wearing braces as a child.

As I grew older I became much more aware of myself, my limitations and my potential. I was determined to unshackle myself from those steel braces and become greater than other students in my class. When I was about nine years old, I took off the braces and began to walk on my own. Although clumsy and awkward at first, I determined to overcome low self-esteem and the sorrow that engulfed my life before then.

My early childhood was filled with fleeting memories of contact with the ghosts of the night. I felt hands moving up and down my body. There was a stir between my legs as the hands moved from one point to another. The night was dark. I could not see a face, I could only feel the hands and soft skin touching me. I could hear increased breathing against my neck. Suddenly I felt a sharp pain between my legs and something hard, yet soft, going inside of me. Slowly my body began to relax and I could feel a strange pleasure flowing through my being and as suddenly as it ended, the person vanished into the darkness.

In the morning when I awoke, I felt a sticky substance that had a strange odor between my legs. My bed was completely wet with yellow urine stains. As my wetting the bed increased, my mother would scold me, sometimes beat me. One morning after I got out of bed drenched in urine, I was shivering in the cold room. The temperature outside was 20 degrees. My mother came into my room screaming and hollering at me. "I'll teach you once and for all, not to wet your bed!" She made me urinate in a drinking glass and told me to drink it. And I did.

The memory of that incident burned deep into my soul. Each time I reflected on it, I got angrier with my mother and the hatred I had for her grew. Many years later, my oldest brother, Sam told me that it was my mother's boyfriend, Oscar, who would sneak into my bedroom at night and molest me; but I never knew for certain. As I grew up, these repressed memories caused me terrible nightmares and constant distrust of people. It was years before I realized the damage from these incidents of molestation. How I survived all these years is truly a miracle!

As a little boy growing up in the Deep South I was fully aware of the Jim Crow laws. I picked cotton in the cotton fields to make extra money to buy food for my family when I was twelve. Picking cotton was not an easy task.

In order to pull the white cotton from its bulb you had to get past the sticky barbs that surrounded the bulb. These barbs would penetrate your fingertips and draw blood. Many evenings after picking cotton, I would come home and my fingers would be bloody and sore. I would be in pain all night. I often found it hard to sleep. I was always thinking about the next day and how I was going to survive.

There were many days when my two brothers, Sam and Sly, and I would go to school with empty stomachs. Food was scarce and most of our meals consisted of beans, okra, greens and pork. Most of our food was grown in the back yard and we raised several pigs for pork meat. We would kill a hog at least twice a year, salt and smoke the meat in the smoke house. Since we needed money to buy clothes, shoes and school supplies, we'd go out into the fields when we were not picking cotton and pick blackberries and plums by the gallon. We would take them to town and sell them to the whites. It was easy and quick money because the white folks loved blackberries and plums. Because of the hazard involved with picking the fruit, they left this job to the us.

Picking blackberries and plums was a risky business. Not only was there the pain of getting stuck by sharp thorns, there was also the danger of running into poisonous snakes. We had to keep an eye out for black water moccasins, coral snakes, rattlesnakes and coach whip. It was rumored that if a coach whip caught you, it would wrap itself around you stick its tail up your nose and whip you until you were dead. Of course this was just a myth, but it was widely believed by blacks, especially the children. One Sunday afternoon while picking berries alone, I ran into a coach whip. He rose up on his tail about twenty-five feet away from me. He was as long as I was tall, maybe longer. At the time, I stood about three feet high. It was looking directly toward me and thought it was trying to hypnotize me. I just stood there struck with fear.

Suddenly I realized that this was just a snake and I was a human being - much smarter than a snake! I had a gallon bucket in one hand and in the other hand I had a glass jar. I took the jar and aimed it at the head of the snake. By some miracle, I struck the snake right on the top of his head. The snake went to the ground. I picked up a tree limb and ran toward it and beat it until it was dead. I never told anyone about this incident, but for the rest of my stay in Mississippi and even until this day I have never forgotten that snake!

Lucille Breland, or Grandma Lucille, as we called her, was a very imposing woman. Half Cherokee and half black, she was the bulwark of the family during our early years in Mississippi. Sam, Sly and Clyde had her last name. Her son, Little Buddy Breland, was thought to be their father. I always had doubts as to whether he was truly their father. I think Mom just gave them Little Buddy's last name. Why she skipped me and gave me the last name of Brown (which is her maiden name) still remains a mystery.

During the day you could always find Grandma Lucille sitting in a rocking chair on the front porch of the white shotgun house in the middle of the block talking to friends. Many people in the neighborhood would stop by just to chat with her. Lucille was very wise and would often tell tales of old Indian folklore and share her knowledge of natural medicine for cures that Indians had passed on to each generation.

Somehow I think I was her favorite. Maybe it was because she knew I would grow up to be gay. I think she knew from the day I was born. She would tell me how my Mom would keep telling her that she wished I had been a girl when I was born. After I was born, friends and neighbors would come by to see me and when they were told I was a boy there allegedly was disbelief written on their faces. They say everyone commented on how I looked just like a girl. After I was sent to reformatory school and later went on to California, I did not see Grandma Lucille until many years later. My mother and my oldest brother, Sam, brought her out to California after she began to suffer from failing health. Almost immediately, she was admitted to Paradise Valley Hospital where she later died. However, I had the opportunity of visiting her just before she died. She did not recognize me. I never saw her again. She died a few weeks later.

My mother sold bootleg whiskey during the war, and one afternoon the sheriff came to our house and questioned my mother. They began to search the house. While she was being questioned, my mother excused herself to go to the outhouse, which was approximately twenty feet from the main house. It was a crudely built toilet with no sewage system. It was merely a hole dug into the ground and a platform built up about two feet above the hole. The shed was built around it.

The sheriff followed my mother to the outhouse and, as she entered, they followed. I stood outside the door and watched them. I saw them begin to wrestle with my mother as she made an attempt to drop something into the toilet. They tore some of her clothes off exposing breasts and were twisting her arms. The image of my mother struggling with the two white sheriffs stuck in my memory for years to come. I began to understand the reality of living in a white dominated society. Not being able to defend those you love from being attacked and abused made me feel like less than a human being. This was the beginning of my hate against a system of unjust laws and discrimination.

As time passed I became more aware of the injustice that lay ahead of me. My early childhood is full of bad memories, broken promises and deferred dreams. A child who did not know his father, dealing with constant rejection by peers, and of course polio were very painful experiences. My effeminate behavior caused girls to tease and boys to shy away from me.

I found myself alone most of the time and especially at school. I had low self-esteem, which caused me to have suicidal ideas.

I constantly questioned the existence of God. I was raised in the church. I attended youth services, prayer meetings and morning and evening Sunday worship. Church was my life. I enjoyed the gospel music and the fire and brimstone sermons. I excelled in youth groups. I won several awards and citations. One award I remember well. It was for reciting all the sixty-six books of the Bible from memory. I have always believed in God, and I still do. When I see rain fall from the sky and the sun shining brightly and upon the earth, the millions of stars brilliantly illuminating the vast universe, the birth of a newborn baby and the miraculous recovery of a terminally ill patient, I know within my heart there is a God. I believe there is a merciful and loving God who cares for us all and especially for me. I must say that the devil has been chasing me all of my life and there were times when there were doubts about my faith in God. Nonetheless, I persevered.

As a little boy I would play with dolls, crochet and knit with the girls in school. At home I would wash all the family clothes, cook and make formula for my baby brother, Clyde. During the annual holidays, like Christmas, Easter and Thanksgiving, my teacher would send me to each classroom and I would draw mural designs on the blackboard depicting that specific holiday. At home I would sketch pictures of the comic book fashion model, Katie Keene, and draw Biblical pictures of Moses, King David and Jesus. I was an aspiring young artist with a natural gift. One day as I was flipping through a comic book, I ran across an interesting advertisement. It said: "Sketch this drawing and win a free art scholarship". I submitted my sketch. About a week later, I was informed that I had won a scholarship to one of America's most famous art schools. When I told my mother she flatly told me that I could not go because I was too young and the school was too far away. For years, I often wondered if I could have become a famous artist like Michelangelo, Rodin, Monet or Picasso.

My childhood innocence was shattered while walking through the white neighborhood coming from school on my way home. As I walked by one house an older man, perhaps in his 50's, was outside working in his front yard. He asked me if I would like to earn some money. I hesitated at first but remembered what my mother said about white folks and how other blacks look up to them. I acknowledged his request and said yes. He gave me a yard rake and told me to rake up the leaves in the front yard and trim some hedges alongside of the house.

After I finished, he invited me into his house to have some cold lemonade. I noticed as we were drinking he was observing me very closely. I became a little nervous. I had heard many stories from older blacks in the neighborhood about white folks and their strange behavior. Even at the age of nine, I was aware of sexual encounters of an unusual nature and I had a strange feeling about what this man was going to do to me. My mother often warned us kids to always do what white folks tell us to do. When the man asked me to go into his bedroom and take my clothes off, I did as he asked. As I lay there in bed naked, I had a strange and morbid feeling that something terrible was going to happen to me. He came to the bed and sat down beside me.

He took his hands and ran them up and down my body and in between my legs. I began to feel some excitement running through my body, and I noticed that my privates were getting hard. Then he reached over and grabbed my private part and massaged it. He then placed my private part into his mouth and I felt a tingling sensation. There was sort of an explosion out of my body. The man then left the room and I got up and I put on my clothes. When he came back into the room, he gave me some money and I left. There was this strange feeling that lingered inside of me as I walked home. I knew I dared not to tell anyone what happened to me. No one would believe me anyway. The memory of this incident has forever left an indelible imprint on my soul.

During my early years in Mississippi, I had intimate contact with not only boys, but also with girls. I started having sex when I was around 9 years old. I remember my first encounter was with a neighborhood girl next door. Her name was Rose and she had three younger sisters, Elaine, Clothier and Diane. There were two younger brothers, June and Carl. I eventually had sex with all of them except June, who was the oldest brother. June and I were pals and we did many things together except have sex. I remember one time we both had sex with his oldest sister, Rose.

One time June and I broke into our school, ransacked all the classrooms and put black ink all over everything. We were caught two days later and had to clean up the mess we were chastised severely. During one of our mischievous outings June, and several other young boys from my neighborhood and I were at a swimming pond near by my house. Everyone was swimming except me. I have always been afraid of water. As a child I would hide under my bed when it rained.

As I stood on the banks watching them swim I noticed June was having problems swimming. We all saw June struggling to stay afloat. Some of the other boys tried to save him but to no avail. I was hopelessly standing at the edge of the pond and realized that I was unable to help him. Even now it hurts to think about it. I never got over losing my best friend and watching the way he died. There was nothing I could do to help him. This incident only reinforced the fear I had for water, and to this day I have never gone swimming.

One day just before my twelfth birthday, while sitting alone daydreaming at school, a young boy about my age came and sat beside me. What is your name, he asked? I said, "Jimmy Ray, and yours?" "Bobby Ray," he replied. I looked at him closer. He was quite a bit taller than I was. He had large brown eyes and a handsome face. As I continued to observe this boy, all kinds of thoughts kept running through my mind. Who is he? I had never seen him before. What does he want? Why is he talking to me? For the last six years that I have been at school no boy has ever sat with me and asked me my name. He asked me where I lived. I answered and told him that I lived across the railroad tracks just west of where we were. He said he lived in Redquarters, a small community East of our school. We talked for a little while and agreed to meet after school. He seemed to have taken a liking to me or had I just imagined it because I had taken a liking to him? When the final bell rang, I ran out of the classroom and out the front entrance of the school. He was there waiting for me.

I was astonished and shocked to see him standing with a smile on his face. He told me that he would walk me halfway home so we could talk some more. As we walked down the steps into the schoolyard I could feel the burning stares of the other kids as we made our way toward the path that led to my house. When I arrived home I was so elated that I forgot to do my chores. My mother came home and she was furious that I had not done what she asked me before she left for work. It always seemed no matter what I did or did not do, my mother never seemed pleased with me and she would take out her frustrations on me. My older brother Sam or my younger brother Sly never seemed to catch the hell that I did and they got away with a lot of mischief that I would not have dared to do. This made me feel estranged from them, "but this day was my day", and I for one was not going to let any of them destroy the sweet sensations I felt for my newfound friend, Bobby Ray. The next day Bobby Ray and I would be the talk of the school. Gossip about us would fill every classroom and every corridor, but to me this did not matter. What did matter is how wonderful it felt to me and how alive it made me feel for the first time in my life.

The next day and for the rest of the school year, we became inseparable from each other, and the gossip about our escapades increased. During recess, lunch and special school events we were always together. The teasing continued, however, we were determined to be together. Our favorite place was an outhouse located on church property between our school and Redquarters. It is here we discovered our most intimate secrets and fulfilled the passions that lay deep in our souls. Who could dare tell or explain to us that little boys do not have sexual relations with each other, that the love we shared is not normal or accepted. We felt this was true love. For the next two years, unbeknownst to our parents, (as far as I knew) we unselfishly, unashamedly shared each others heart, soul and body and remained deeply committed to each other.

The dream of Bobby Ray's and mine was destined to come to an end sooner or later, even to innocent young boys playing in a world of make believe. It happened one summer afternoon. It was Sunday in a densely vegetated field with tall southern pine trees and the sweet intoxicating smell of honeysuckle vines. There another friend and I were lying buck-naked on soft pine needles fondling each other passionately. The sunlight filtering through the tall pine trees danced softly upon his pale slender body contrasting the ebony hue of mine. And this was in stark contrast to the age old taboo of black and white mixing in the deep south.

As we lay there spent of our passions, we heard noises and people talking coming directly toward us. I turned and looked toward the noises and I saw three white men. I jumped up, grabbed my clothes and started running as fast as I could. I didn't stop until I was on the other side of the field - where I "belonged" in the colored area. Still naked, I stopped just long enough to put my clothes back on. I was shaking with fear, wondering what would have happened if they had caught me, so I kept running until I arrived home. I went into the house and changed my clothes. I stayed in the house believing they were probably looking for me.

Later that afternoon I noticed two black cars patrolling the area around the neighborhood. I knew now that they were indeed looking for me and I was scared to death. No one in my family knew what had happened. No one was home. I had no father and there was no one else to turn to for help. I stayed in the house fearing for my life knowing that something drastic would probably happen to me if they caught me. I remembered the cold-blooded murder of 13-year-old Emmett Till by white men for just whistling at a white girl. Seeing the gruesome newspaper photos of Emmett Till's body pulled from the river was repugnant and distressing to me. Here I was, now facing a similar situation and wondering what was going to happen to my family and me.

I remembered that I had to attend Sunday evening services, and if I didn't, I would catch hell and a possible beating from my mother. Around 6:00 P.M., I began to get dressed in the same clothes I had worn earlier, knowing that if I changed into different clothes it would cause suspicion. But on the other hand, dressing in the same clothes would be recognizable by the police looking for me. After dressing I went into the backyard and as I was talking to a friend of mine across the fence. I heard screeching tires and before I could react, I saw two men running towards me. I stood there in shock as they grabbed me by my arms and led me to the awaiting police cars. I noticed in one of the cars they had my friend sitting between two other men. They put me in the other car and both cars sped off toward town.

I was taken to the town administration building and was interrogated by three police officers. I was threatened with an injection of truth serum after denying the accusations. I explained what really happened and that the relationship between the two of us was mutual, I was slapped very hard across the face by one of the officers. After hours of interrogation, I finally confessed to everything. I was forced to sign a confession whereupon I was then taken to the jail across the street and locked into a single cell. Here I was, barely 13 years old and sitting in a jail cell alone without any visitors, not knowing the whereabouts of my mother, brothers or other family members.

The next day my mother was allowed to visit me. She was very concerned but still angry with me. I could see the pain and fear in her face. When she left she told me not to talk to anyone. That evening, my grandmother Lucille came to visit me. I told her exactly what had happened. She listened attentively shaking her head from side to side. Finally she said she believed me. She told me not to talk to anyone and assured me they would get me released. As she was about to leave, an officer came into the cell with a tray of food. After the officer left, she warned me not to eat the food. She pointed out a bluish color to the mashed potatoes and explained that the potatoes contained poison. I immediately took the tray and dumped its contents into the commode. She went home and brought me some food. The next day I was released.

Soon I was placed on a bus going to Louisiana. My mother explained to me just before the bus arrived that I was going to Louisiana to stay with my Aunt Bette in Poncestula, and from there I would move with her to San Diego, California. I was told however, that I would have to come back to Wiggins, Mississippi, when my case was heard by the court.

When I arrived at my aunt's house in Louisiana, she was very happy to see me but also very concerned about my legal situation. I told her everything. She was sympathetic and told me not to worry. Three weeks later the three of us, Aunt Bette, her husband, and I, left for California,. We arrived in San Diego in the middle of the summer of 1956. This was my first time in California and, the little brown people called Mexicans fascinated me. I was transformed into a new world of "technicolor", a unique blend of brown, yellow, red, black and white people all working together, going to school together and living together. Each day I learned something new about the people, food, places, and about the different religions that were practiced I was amazed how well these people seemed to get along with each other and how the children mixed and mingled without any fear of racial tension or legal ramifications. My stay in San Diego was ephemeral.

Several weeks after I arrived, my aunt told me I had to return to Mississippi. The next day after arriving back in Wiggins, I was taken to the town courthouse where I pled guilty to the charges as was previously agreed. I was immediately placed in a reformatory school outside of Jackson, Mississippi for an indefinite amount of time to be decided by the school officials.

My first night at the reformatory school was a date with the devil, a night in hell -- a night I will never forget as long as I live. I was assigned to a dorm that housed about seventy other young boys ranging in age from 10 to 18 years old. There were seven rooms without doors. Each room housed approximately twelve boys. I was placed in the last room at the end of the hall with ten other boys. When the lights went out for the night I was approached by several boys, some from the other rooms of the dorm. Two of them grabbed me, while another boy began to undress me. As I lay there naked on my stomach, held by the same two boys, I was raped repeatedly by one boy after another until I passed out from all the rough penetration inflicted upon me. I never could have imagined what it would be like to be forced to have sex with, especially with several people, repeatedly.

I was awakened the next morning by the house parent. There was nobody else in the room except the house parent and myself. I was still naked and I could smell and feel the sperm between my legs. My whole body felt like a ton of bricks. I was so weak from exhaustion that I could hardly get up from the bed. The house parent told me to take a shower, and I headed to the shower room. Just as I finished my shower, the house parent came into the room with a long leather belt with three-square holes at the end. He told me to bend over and he gave me several lashes on my wet, naked ass and told me never to let it happen again.

After the incident I once again found myself alone. I kept to myself most of the time until several days later, a young boy with the prettiest green eyes walked up to me and began a conversation. As we talked, I became mesmerized by his appearance. He was taller than I was, with a slender build, golden brown skin, curly hair and hypnotic green eyes. Perhaps you can say it was love at first sight. I felt a deep emotional feeling for him, and that day we became lovers.

It was an unwritten code among the inmates of the school to have someone as a lover to protect you from other boys. He was my protector and we shared each other's dreams and undivided love for each other. This love affair continued until I was paroled after about a year of incarceration. I was paroled to San Diego, California where my mother and three brothers, Sam, Sly and Clyde had already moved.

During my stay at Oakley Training School, the reformatory school where I was sent for having an affair with a young white boy, I attended an off-ground public school. I went to school with kids that were not from the reformatory. This public school was called Utica Institute. We would be picked up each day and bussed to the Institute from reformatory school. I made very good grades while at Utica Institute and enjoyed the freedom of being around kids who were not from the reformatory. My most memorable time there was when I joined the marching band. I couldn't march with a cello so I switched to the xylophone, but for reasons I still do not understand that didn't work out either.

One day the coach of the marching band approached me and he said, "You are a very unusual person," (I think he was referring to my feminine qualities or perhaps my feminine behavior) and he suggested I become a drum major. So I began to practice and became the drum major for the entire band. That worked out perfectly! Another memorable event at Utica was attending a showing of the movie, "Carrie". I was very shocked! I was totally devastated after watching this movie. I said to myself, "How could anyone be that cruel to another person?" I guess in some way I was identifying with Carrie and reflecting on the attacks I endured. Eventually I had to leave Utica Institute because I was paroled from the reformatory school and sent home to my mother in California.

CHAPTER TWO

In 1957, San Diego was just a small, sleepy Navy town. The area known today as Mission Valley was nothing but farmland. You could see sheep, goats and cows grazing along the mountains and the slopes below. The tallest building, about ten stories high, was the El Cortez Hotel that sat on top of a hill in downtown San Diego. Downtown itself was a cluster of small shops, coffee shops, restaurants and arcades. There were several hotels and motels. The two largest hotels besides the El Cortez were the US Grant Hotel across from Horton Plaza and the San Diego Hotel west on Broadway. I arrived back in San Diego in December of 1957 from Oakley and started high school.

San Diego High School looked like a prison from the outside. It had an appropriate nickname, "The Old Gray Castle". In 1957 at the age of sixteen, I started as an eleventh-grader at San Diego High school. My first day at school was a total disaster. It brought back memories of my childhood days at Stone County Training School in Mississippi. Boys began to call me a sissy and the girls would make fun of me and tease me about my feminine behavior. During the next several months, I was unable to concentrate on my studies. I was involved in a fight at least once a day. I was called "Mississippi" because of my southern accent. There was no end to the derogatory comments or the terrible humiliation I faced on a daily basis.

One day while I was taking a shower after gym class, three boys approached and attempted to rape me. I fought back and lucky for me, some other boys came into the shower room. When the three boys saw them they split. I reported the incident to the counselor's office. The next day I was transferred out of the gym class and into the R.O.T.C. class. For the next several days, I became the talk of the school. They said things like, "Mississippi was raped in gym class and transferred to R.O.T.C.," "The fag was caught having sex in the gym shower with several boys."

Finally, I had enough! My grades were poor. I had to fight my way to school and back home. I couldn't sleep at night wondering what I would have to endure the next day. I requested a transfer to another school and ended up at Snyder Continuation School across from San Diego High on Twelfth Avenue. It was a school for problem students. The students that attended Snyder were considered misfits, incorrigibles and having some form of antisocial behavior. I became one of those students and ironically found myself more socially accepted than I had been at San Diego High School. That same year I met other young gay guys and began to socialize with them.

I would dress in tight pants and wear a calypso shirt opened in front and tied around the midriff. I wore makeup and my hair was pressed. I was entering a new phase of my sexuality. The incidents and tragedies of the past began to shape my future. Of course, I didn't have the faintest idea what life had in store for me. How could I possibly know!

One day while heading home from school, I was walking down a hill on National Avenue, east of 30th Street. There were a couple of houses to my right and between these two houses was a vacant lot before you got to the next structure. I heard footsteps behind me and as I turned I saw four young black males, much older than I was. They walked up to me. One of them pushed me down the hill, and they all attacked me. Two of them held me while one sexually assaulted me. Eventually each one of them sexually assaulted me. They left me there half naked. I pulled myself up to the street level, picked up my tattered clothing and got dressed. I was shocked and in a trance-like state. I had been violated, completely taken advantage of. I did not know what to do. I knew what they did was wrong but I had no one to tell. I couldn't tell my mother. She wouldn't believe me. I couldn't tell my stepfather because he was already abusing me. I thought about telling the police, but they wouldn't believe me either. So I lived with it. I suppressed it. I had been raped. Later on, I would rationalize to myself, if they had asked me to have sex with them I probably would have. But to force me was something different. I could not understand. I could not accept it.

During the same year, 1957, I had my first encounter with the law. I was sent to juvenile hall twice for leading an immoral life. After that, I was sent to Atascadero State Hospital on two different occasions for a ninety-day evaluation as a sexual psychopath. Both times I was released as not being amenable to treatment. Since I was not amenable to treatment, it was determined that I was not a sexual psychopath. Atascadero State Hospital was quite an experience. I was housed on a ward with approximately fifty other patients, all of who had different types of mental problems. I must admit that I was afraid of the people around me. There was one patient who would walk back and forth every day, talking loudly, pointing his finger toward the ceiling, cussing and saying, "You bitch! I will kill you!" Over and over again he would shout toward this imaginary being until the attendants took him away to his room for the night. There was another patient who believed that he was Jesus Christ. He would religiously walk around the main yard all day with a white turban on his head with his hands pressed together as though he were praying to God. I was there for a ninety-day observation during which I was given several tests. I also had several one-on-one sessions with a psychiatrist. About two weeks before my ninety days were up, my ward doctor informed me that I would be released and sent back to court.

While at Atascadero State Hospital I was treated like a queen. Guys of all races would bring me gifts and do special favors for my attention. Being only sixteen, I was one of the three youngest patients there. It was at the hospital that I began to learn the power I possessed. Some people call it sex appeal, I call it magnetism. I simply had a certain charm that was irresistible to most men. My provocative walk, enticing looks, alluring smile and effeminate mannerisms were intoxicating to these little boys who came to the playground (too engaged in activities to prove how foolish they were). I may not have been a sexual psychopath, but after spending a short time there, I became confused and mentally disturbed by the environment. I began to believe that I was abnormal, and it seemed no one care d about me. I wondered if someday I would end up like some of those others at Atascadero and spend the rest of my life in a nut house talking to myself.

On my second admission to Atascadero State Hospital, again for masquerading, I met a young French boy. He had flaming, fire engine red hair. He was there on a sex charge. We were on the same ward together and immediately we became friends. We both worked in the culinary department. We went to movies together, played games together and watched TV together. It was he who gave me the name Charmagne and that name stuck. Later on I earned the first part of my name, which was Princess. That's how Princess Charmagne came into being. After I left Atascadero State Hospital the second time, I would often wonder what happened to this young man who gave birth to Princess Charmagne.

After returning to San Diego, I reentered San Diego High School but spent most of my time running up and down the streets of downtown San Diego. I would stay at friends' houses and sometimes I would spend all night hanging out at the coffee shops. Ferris and Ferris was one of my favorite coffee houses because it stayed open all night and it was a very good place for picking up dates and making money. It was during one of these nights while hanging out at Prixie's Coffee Shop that I was arrested for leading an immoral life, and I was taken to a Juvenile Hall. I spent several weeks at Juvenile Hall before I was sent to CYA.

One night while roaming the streets of downtown San Diego, an older gentleman picked me up and took me to his home in La Jolla. It was a beautiful home in the village of La Jolla on the Pacific Coast. After our sexual interlude, we talked for a while. He appeared to be very lonely and was looking for someone with whom to have some sort of relationship. He told me he owned a clothing store on Fifth Avenue in San Diego. We started out having an open relationship where I would see him several times a week. I visited his store several times downtown. He gave me a special card to purchase clothes at his store. Later he gave me a credit card in my name. Since I was only seventeen years old and had no job, he co-signed the credit agreement. He also opened an account in my name at Walker Scott, one of the largest department stores on Broadway in San Diego. He paid all the bills on these accounts. Our relationship continued for the next several years until I went to CYA for masquerading. While I was in CYA, I lost contact with him and have never seen him again.

My first incarceration was in March 1959. I was sent to Preston School of Industry (CYA) for living an immoral life and being a danger to myself and to society. This was my first time being locked up for a long period of time since leaving reformatory school in Mississippi. Unlike the Oakley Training School in Mississippi, Preston was a strange world filled with young boys, ranging in age from 12 to 21. The boys at Preston School of Industry were quite an assortment of nationalities, races and backgrounds. I found myself in the midst of a fantasy world; a unique playground for a young black homosexual queen whose sexual desires were running rampant. I was housed in a unit with approximately sixty other boys about my age. During the day we mingled together in the dayroom, dining room, library and in educational and athletic activities. Each unit had an inmate leader called unit corporal. He is supposed to be the toughest and the "baddest" inmate in the group. There was always someone who wanted to challenge the leader. One day the unit leader and I got into an argument about my behavior, which led to a fight. I got the best of him and many in the group wanted me to become unit leader, but I was refused the position by the company officer due to my homosexuality. It wouldn't be good for the morale of the company in the eyes of the other companies on campus. Nevertheless, from that day on, I received a lot of respect from my fellow inmates. By some strange turn of events, the inmate I got into the fight with later became my lover, and we continued our affair until I was paroled on February 9, 1960.

I was paroled from Preston Industry, California Youth Authority, to my mother in San Diego, California. My mother was remarried and my new stepfather's name was Bill Green. Everything seemed to be fine and I had great optimism about my future. I enrolled in school, and I had a girlfriend. I decided to make a promise to myself that I would change my life and be somebody. My girlfriend was named Bernice and she knew about my past life. However, had no effect on her feelings for me because she was a lesbian.

One day Bernice and I were out walking down Broadway walking in front of the US Grant Hotel. We were on our way to the Spreckles

Theatre on 1st Ave. We attended a movie, and after the movie we went home. The next day my girl friend, Bernice, came over to my place and told me that she wanted to introduce me to someone. That afternoon she came back to my place and she had with her a young girl about 16 years old who had flaming red hair and blue eyes. Bernice said, "I want you to meet Elizabeth", who, she said, was a lesbian. She introduced me as Princess Charmagne. Unbeknown to me at the time, Elizabeth was under the assumption that I was a real woman. That is the reason she wanted to meet me. She told me later that she had seen Bernice and I walking down Broadway and that she had asked Bernice to introduce her to me. We partied that night and later on ended up back at my place where she spent the night. That is when she discovered that I was a man. This did not change her mind about being with me!

For the next several months we lived together and shared our passion and our dreams. She was fun and we were happy together. It might have been a permanent arrangement if it had not been for her family. We would go out together to coffee shops, restaurants and parties and I would continue to prostitute. One day I came home and Miss Norman who lived down the hall from me told me that the police had come by and had taken Elizabeth. I later found out that her father, who was a prominent businessman in the community had hired a detective to find her. When the detective found her and reported back to her father, her father was furious and sent the police to get her because she was under 18. I also later found out that he told the police that he did not appreciate his daughter living with a black man who wore women's clothes.

They took Elizabeth to the county mental health department. After she was admitted I got a chance to visit her once. The next time I tried to visit her, they told me I could not see her. I discovered later that they had transferred her out of the mental health department into a private facility. I never saw her again. I often wonder about her and what happened to her. I remember one time when we were together she took me by her father's house, but I did not go in. I waited for her outside. Once after she was admitted to the private mental facility, I went by her father's home again and stood outside for a short time and then left. Many years have passed since that day and I am quite sure that the family does not live there anymore. Maybe someday I will see her again, and I hope that she remembers me. She was my only heterosexual relationship, although I have slept with many women over the years.

Once again, fate would step in and run my life. One Sunday morning my stepfather was taking my mother to church and my other brothers were out playing somewhere in the neighborhood. I was alone in the house when my stepfather returned. I was in the kitchen cooking and he approached me and made inappropriate advances toward me. I was not aware of Bill's eyes following my every move and was completely surprised when Bill propositioned me. When I hesitated in my reply to Bill's demands, he threatened me. He said he would tell my mother that I made advances to him. He went on to tell me if I didn't do what he wanted me to do, he would put me out of the house, and I would end up going back to CYA. I didn't want to go back to Preston. I hated that place where I had been locked up most of the time and my opportunity to have sexual affairs was limited. I finally gave in to my stepfather's demands. It was a painful decision to make, but it appeared to me that I had no choice. I was still on parole from CYA. This affair lasted for several months, taking place only when my mother was away from the house and no one else was around.

One evening while in downtown San Diego, I ran into a friend of mine named Mario. We had attended San Diego High School together and he informed me that his mother had thrown him out of the house. He had no place to go. That night I took him home with me. I snuck him into the house and into the bedroom where I slept with one of my brothers. Mario slept in the same bed with me that night. The next morning, I awakened and made sure that he was covered so that nobody would see him. Unfortunately, my mother came into the room, perhaps to wake my other brother up to go to school, and she discovered Mario in my bed. She approached me about it, I told her that he didn't have any place to go and I let him stay here. She started screaming at me, calling me names like queer, whore and slut. I became very angry. That's when I told her about Bill, my stepfather, and what he had been doing to me. She stalked out of the room screaming that she didn't believe me; that I was lying. She went into the kitchen and got a butcher knife and returned to the bedroom and tried to stab me. I had to defend myself. By that time, Mario was leaving the room and I managed to escape out the door behind him.

We both ended up on the streets. For the next two years, I was on the streets. I slept in doorways, parked cars, and vacant houses, and I stole food from stores. I hustled on the streets of downtown San Diego, at the Plaza, by going home with older men for money. Eventually, I ran into an older "queen" who offered to let me stay at his house. He was a drag queen who dressed in women's clothes and soon had me dressing in women's clothes, too. For the next five years, I lived as Princess Charmagne.

Miss Duchess was the first drag queen I met when I ran away from home to escape my abusive stepfather. After spending about two years on the streets I ran into Miss Duchess at Prixie's Coffee shop on 5th Ave.

Late one night about three o'clock in the morning, she came into the coffee shop. She was an older queen. She came to our table with another queen by the name of Miss Willie Givens. She wanted to know why we young queens were still out on the streets that late at night. In a joking way, I responded I was out there because I had nowhere else to go. She said, "My dear, if you don't have a place to go you can come and stay with me". So I moved in with her the next day, and I stayed for about six months. She was very kind to me, and taught me how to dress, and how to wear makeup. She also gave me advice on how to stay out of trouble with the police. Miss Duchess is still alive as of this writing.

In the early sixties, San Diego became a haven for prostitutions, peep shows, massage parlors, and organized crimes. The San Diego Police Department was infested with corrupt cops, many of them including vice officers were on the take. Organized crime had taken over the massage and gambling business. Among the crimes corruption and chaos was a beautiful prostitute named Shirley. She was hot, and her services were in high demand. I met Shirley Fargo one night at the Crossroads Club on Fourth and Market Street. I was sitting at the bar with a glass of champagne in my hand when I almost fell off the barstool. I was shocked, stunned. I could not believe my eyes. It was like looking into a mirror and seeing myself. She looked just like me. When she saw me, she too was equally surprised at the resemblance we shared. That night we became the best of friends.

Later, we came to realize that our looking alike had a disadvantage The police or vice cops, had on numerous occasions mistaken me for her and vice versa. Shirley had already established a reputation as the best-dressed whore in the red light district. Her reputation was highly regarded by other whores, pimps and players. It was inevitable that I would build an equal reputation because of my resemblance to Shirley and my tenacious ambition to be the best. One night while strolling down Fifth Avenue from Pixie Coffee Shop, I was stopped by town vice officers. They had mistaken me for Shirley and were about to arrest me when they discovered my State Identification - my true identity. The vice cops were amazed at my resemblance to Shirley. Since I was the new kid on the block, this was their first encounter with me. They asked me my drag name and told them Charmagne. After they finished their interrogation, they explained why they stopped me. They thought I was Shirley and they were looking for her for clipping a sailor. Before they left in their unmarked car, they warned they would be keeping an eye on me.

I had been warned about vice cops and their tactics of using prostitutes to obtain information in exchange for not harassing or arresting them. I had heard that Shirley was hooked up with a sergeant on the police force.

Whenever necessary and when it was within his power he would pull strings to get her out of jail or having charges dropped. This was not an uncommon practice during this time in San Diego. There were other prostitutes, drag queens, drug dealers and mobsters who had some degree of juice with the police department. I was standing on the corner of Fifth and Market in front of Farris and Farris Coffee shop around midnight when a black and white police car pulled to the curb. A very young handsome policeman got out of the car. He had gold bars on his shoulder and gold stripes on his sleeves. He approached me. Suddenly he stopped and said, "You're not Shirley." I replied, "No, I am Princess Charmagne." I knew then that he was the sergeant in Shirley's life.

The first and the fifteenth of each month was payday for all servicemen. Prostitutes, drag queens, pimps, whores, hustlers and con artists alike lived for those two days! Sailors in their white, tight uniforms showing their enormous basket and spending money like their was no tomorrow. Those who just reenlisted had several hundred dollars in their wallets. Many of them would end up so intoxicated they would become a victim of a "roll" and end up the next morning broke. I rolled many sailors and ended up with three or four thousand dollars on the first and fifteenth of each month. Shirley and I would always see which one of us ended up with the most money. Sometimes she would score more than I. We always had fun competing with each other. My reputation was building fast. It was rumored among the "Who's Who" in the red light district that Princess Charmagne made more money in one night than three `real" whores in two nights.

I wore women's clothes twenty-four hours a day. I became a well-known prostitute in the red light district, which consisted of Fifth Avenue and Market Street in downtown San Diego. I frequented such clubs as The Crossroads, The Zebra Club, The Jolly Inn, The Shalimar, The Bucket of Blood, The Black and Tan Club, and Kiddio #1 and Kiddio #2, the Cheechee Club (which is still there) and Bradley's. I would pick up many sailors, sometimes marines, businessmen. There were times when I would pick up foreign military personnel and take them home on dates. I made money by charging them anywhere from $100-200. I didn't realize the power I had over the men until I would get them into bed, sometimes three at a time. They seemed to be so focused on self gratification that they didn't realize or they overlooked the fact that I was a man. I learned how to manipulate them while they were in a euphoric, lustful state. I would take their penis and place it into my rectum, and they thought they were having sex with a woman, never realizing that I was a man. Some of these dates continued to come back again and again. During this time, I didn't really like what I was doing, but I was convinced I was doing it out of necessity (I really had wanted to be a Clarence Darrow, a famous criminal attorney!) These men would pass the word to their friends. I made so much money that I would throw parties about three times a week at my apartment.

By this time I was so well known in San Diego, that people would come from all over to attend my parties. They came from Del Mar, Mission Beach, El Cajon and all the other surrounding areas. Lawyers, doctors and other prominent people in the community who were "in the closet" attended these parties. The parties became very popular among the military personnel, especially sailors. They really didn't know I was a man! Women attended the parties as well, heterosexuals, prostitutes - you name it! People from all sexual preferences attended my parties.

I was living the life of a high-class prostitute. I had one objective and that was to control the men that I was involved with. I had vowed as a kid when I first saw my mother abused by her boyfriend, that I would never allow a man to control me. At this point I swore I would use anything in my power to degrade them, to abuse them, to discredit them and to control them. There were times I had dates with men to whom I revealed my true but secret identity. I let them know I was not a woman but a man. During the course of these encounters, I would get these individuals so drunk that after they would have sex with me, I would have sex with them as a man. I truly believe that my obsession was mainly the result of my feelings against my stepfathers and mother who abused me.

From 1960 to 1964, I spent my life as a prostitute having constant confrontation with the police. Each night was a night to remember. Sailors in their white, tight pants were a sight to remember. When anyone asked me what was my favorite food was, I would always say "Seafood". In the glow of the orange sunset Sailors of all races, colors and nationality walked down the streets seeking nightlife pleasures, and there I stood, Princess Charmagne, in the midst of heaven and hell, enjoying the attention. Each night I would pick up several sailors, some from here, others from other countries. I made approximately $500 to $600 dollars a night and averaged $3,000 to $5,000 thousand a week. I had more money than I ever had in my life. This was more than I could have ever imagined. The exhilaration and excitement of meeting young sailors and having fun with them and making money, a lot of money, at the same time! This almost made me forget about the abusive memories of my past and the unforgettable period of my life when I slept in vacant houses and parked cars. I was having the time of my life. I had earned the reputation among friends, whores and pimps as the best moneymaker on Fifth Ave. There was one drag queen that gave me a run for my money. Her name was Miss Nicole.

She was very pretty dressed in drag, a light-skinned black with green eyes. We were very competitive in defending our reputation as the best moneymakers in the Red Light District.

One night Nicole picked up two jarheads (Marines) and took them to her hotel room. The next day the hotel manager found her body. Both of her eyes had been punched out and there was massive trauma to the rest of her body. The police later arrested her killers, two jarheads, and charged them with murder. The murder made front page news in San Diego. It was said that when the two marines found out that she was a man, instead of a woman, they became angry and killed her. For the next several weeks her death was "talk-of-the-town" among the people involved in the Gas-lamp District nightlife.

This incident was a wake-up call, not only for me, but also for the rest of the drag queens, prostitutes and hustlers. Prostitution is a dangerous and sometimes deadly game. Back in the day you had to be good to survive. I kept away from Marines because I knew their reputation as being gung ho and macho. My clients consisted mostly of young sailors. Sailors were more unique, meek, timid and carefree. One out of every five sailors I met was either green around the ears or bi-sexual. Even to this day I remember Nicole with her pretty green eyes and affectionate smile. I often thank God for watching over me.

However, I did have a few encounters with a Marine. One happened at the Coast Hotel, the same hotel where I was later shot by my Navy lover. I picked this Marine up at a bar on Fifth Avenue and took him to the hotel room I had rented for the night. Once we were in bed he began to run his hand between my legs. I was still wearing my girdle. Suddenly he stopped and jumped out of the bed, cussing and saying, "You are a man!" When I attempted to get out of the bed he grabbed me, and we began to struggle. I pushed him forward as I reached for the door. I opened the door and he followed me out, still in his underwear. He grabbed me again, yelling loud at the same time. Perhaps it was lucky for me that the room I rented was right across from the hotel manager's apartment. The manager was a friend of mine. He heard all the yelling and came to his door with a gun. He pointed the gun at the Marine and told him to stop. The Marine went back into the room, and

I split. The shooting that later happened to me at this same hotel and the current incident brought me even closer to becoming a statistic in my career as a prostitute. Soon there would be another.

One night while at the Jolly Inn, sitting in a booth talking to two sailors and a friend, I was approached by a lady who began to yell at me, cussing, saying that I was having an affair with her husband. She pulled out a gun and pointed it at me. I was very afraid that she might pull the trigger. I remained silent and everyone in the club was very quiet, too. Finally she told me that she blamed her husband as much as she blamed me. I told her I didn't know who her husband was. I promised her it would never happen again.

She relaxed and finally put the gun back into her purse and walked out of the Club. Everyone in the Club wanted to know who her husband was. It wasn't long after that news spread of Princess Charmagne having been threatened by a woman accusing him of having an affair with a her husband.

Later on I would run into a married couple who owned several pieces of property and a business near Fifth and Market. They were older and well respected. They were an inter-racial couple, and I think the husband was bisexual. He seemed to take a liking to me. Later I would find out that his wife was also bisexual. They owned one club called the Kiddio Club and they wanted to open another and have me run it for them. Since I was still underage and could not purchase a license to sell alcohol, they got the license in their name. We called the new nightclub Kiddio Two. I ran the nightclub for the next couple of years. I was there every night. My name became even more famous because a lot of people, especially servicemen and some of the younger set, would patronize this club. It was here that I would meet a lot of my dates and take them home for the night. It was also at this club that I picked up my first felony - getting marijuana for a friend.

Events in my life often gave way to myths that everyone wanted to believe. One particular rumor was that someone had said I had married a sergeant in the police department in National City while dressed in drag. The rumor persists even to this day, but I never married a police officer or anyone else.

I can't imagine how the marriage rumor got started. Maybe it started with an affair that I had had with a foreign serviceman who was an official in the Honduran Navy. I met this man one night at the Spanish Village and he thought I was a woman. That first night, he bought me all kinds of drinks and told me how beautiful I was and that he wanted to go home with me. I did not take him home so he told me he would like to see me again since he was going to be in town for a few weeks. I told him I was always somewhere around Fifth and Market at one of the clubs, and that's where he could surely find me. The next night I was sitting in The Crossroads club listening to some jazz when he walked in with a couple of friends from his country. He was dressed in a Navy uniform. We talked, and for the rest of the night we went out clubbing and having fun. Again, he wanted to go home with me, and again I told him no.

At the time I met him, I was already involved in a relationship with another American Navy guy, and I was not interested in having an affair with anyone else. I knew that if I took him home it would not be a one-night stand because of his intense interest in me. The following night I was at the Zebra Club when he came in.

He walked up to me and pulled out a little case he had in his pocket. He opened it. Inside was a gold ring with a diamond in the center. He gave it to me and asked me to marry him. I looked at him quizzically, not knowing what to say. I told him that I would have to think about it. All the time, it I was wondering how I could pull this off. To me, life has always been a challenge and this would be one of the greatest challenges I would have taken, so far. Was I willing to risk jeopardizing my freedom by marrying another man, especially when I knew it was illegal? I kept the ring for several days and finally returned it to him. I told him I could not marry him. He was very disappointed but I kept seeing him until he finally went back to Honduras. He never knew I was not a woman. The day before he left he gave me another ring. It was a gold ring with a unique symbol in the center that resembled a lion. He told me to keep the ring as a remembrance of him. I kept it for many years until one day it was stolen.

I remember one night after I had "gotten off work" I was tired. I had made several hundred dollars that night. It was about 3:00 in the morning and I was sitting in Ferris and Ferris. I was sitting at the counter sipping a cup of coffee when a man walked in and sat down beside me. He was well dressed and wearing a very expensive tie. He asked me what I was doing. I told him that I was on my way home. He propositioned me and I told him I was sorry, I was tired and I needed to go home to get some rest. He continued to talk to me and tried to persuade me to go his hotel room. He told me he was a businessman here from the East Coast. When I realized that he was not going to give up trying to get me to go to his hotel with him, I turned and looked him in the eye and said, "Listen sir, what you see is not what you really see ... I'm not a woman, I'm a man"! He looked at me and said, "I don't believe it"! You are too beautiful to be a man. I said, "It's true ... I am a man." He said, "I'll tell you what I will do. I will give you $500 right now, in cash, if you will go up to my hotel room with me. If you can prove that you are not a woman, you can keep the $500 and leave." He reached in his pocket, pulled out his wallet, gave me $500 in $20 dollar bills. I went with him and got into his car. He drove to the U.S. Grant Hotel downtown on Broadway and we went up to his room. I walked in behind him and closed the door. He said, "Now prove to me you're not a woman." I pulled up my dress and pulled down my girdle and my panties. He said, "I'll be damned, I don't believe it! You are too beautiful to be a man! Keep the money. You can go."

Sabrina Rubalcava and Clarence Francois were both drag queens. Sabrina was Indian, Spanish, and black --- a very pretty queen whom I met at the Zebra Club. We were very close friends. We did a lot of things together; worked the streets, night clubbed and lived in the same apartment complex.

She made a lot of money having dates with sailors and marines. She always seemed to have a steady companion. She would participate in the annual Miss Black San Diego Pageant that was held at the Elk's Club. Then there was Miss Francois, whom we called Frances. She was half-black and half-French. She was another pretty queen about my age. We were much closer than Sabrina and I, probably because of the age difference. It seemed that every time I got in trouble, Frances got in trouble. We would usually end up going to juvenile hall together. Then there was Miss Bert. Miss Bert was about Sabrina's age. Perhaps she was three to four years older than Miss Frances and I. Miss Bert would treat us like we were her daughters. Miss Bert was not really a pretty queen except when she had her makeup on. When she finished making up and getting dressed, it was very hard to tell she was not a woman.

Frances and I had been running buddies every since we were 15 years old. He lived with his mother, Delores. He did not have a father, and his mother would allow him to express his sexuality. She would buy him nice clothes, most of them very feminine, and he would wear lots of makeup. During the evening we would go downtown and hang out at Horton Plaza. Because we were under 21, we could not get into the bars at the time. So we frequented coffee shops and hung out on street corners. We would often visit older queens at their homes. One day we left home and went to a friend of ours named Miss Duchess. We spent two days at Miss Duchess's house. My mother and Frances' mother were looking for us. When they could not find us, they called the police. Someone had told them that they had seen us at Miss Duchess's house. The police came to the house and took us into custody and threatened to file charges against Miss Duchess for contributing to the delinquency of a minor. The police placed us in the custody of our mothers. My mother was furious with me when I got home. I went into my room and closed the door. I did not feel like arguing with her. I did not believe she really cared about me anyway.

Frances and I continued to run up and down town. Sometimes we would go to clothing stores and shoplift. We would steal expensive cocktail dresses, mini skirts, leather coats and fine jewelry. We were very good at this. But, of course, one day we got caught and ended up going to juvenile hall. We spent about three weeks at juvenile hall before being released back to our mothers. We continued our escapades together - shoplifting, picking up young sailors, taking them to our friend's house and going to Tijuana and having a ball. We always dressed nice and we were very noticeable as gays by others who saw us on the streets.

We would have trouble with some young guys who did not like gays and when they called us names like queer and faggot we would fight them. We always stood up for what we believed in, and we never backed down from a fight.

Miss Sabrina Rubalcava and I met around 1959. He, Miss Frances, Miss June and I worked the streets in what was then called the Red Light District. Back then the district was located south to Island Ave, north to F Street, East to Twelfth Street and West to First Street. Today it is called the Gaslamp Quarter. Miss Sabrina became a good friend, second only to Miss Frances. Miss Sabrina and I had a great deal in common. We were the only two drag queens at that time who dressed in women's clothes 24-hours a day. Other queens would only dress in women's clothes occasionally and other times they would appear in public in semi-drag (makeup on, tight pants and calypso shirt or woman's blouse with no bra, etc.) Miss Sabrina lived in the same hotel complex as I did. She would pick up dates and take them home and turn tricks. She was very good at what she did, but perhaps I was even better. She would come to all my parties and sometimes we would hang out together after hours at either Ferris and Ferris or Prixie's Coffee Shop. When he was dressed in women's clothes and had applied all his makeup, he looked just like a real woman. There were a few people who knew that she was a man, but most were unaware of her sexual identity. Just by looking at her you could not tell what she really was.

I remember one time I had taken a Marine up to the hotel that Miss Sabrina managed. While at the hotel turning a trick with the marine, I discovered that he had over $3,000 on him. When we finished I left him in the room but I had his money stashed in my bra. Sabrina would tell me later that as I went down the stairs to the sidewalk that I had dropped money all the way down the steps. After about five minutes the police were all over the place. The next morning detectives came to my hotel room, knocked on the door, and I opened it. They asked if they could come in. I said yes, be my guest. They asked me where I had been the previous night. I told them I really didn't know. They questioned me some more about my whereabouts and wanted to search my room. I asked them if they had a search warrant, and they said no. Then I politely asked them to leave. They left. I later on found out that the marine was so drunk that he did not remember who he was with or how much money he had, so the police really did not have a case.

Sabrina and I remained close friends over the years. We were in prison twice about the same time. Each time she got out of prison and I was out, we continued to drag. When I was paroled from prison in 1974, I went back to San Diego. I worked for a while in construction. I saved my money and opened up a record and gift shop on 43rd and University Avenue. Later on that year, Miss Sabrina was paroled from Vacaville Medical Facility and I let her stay at my apartment. I also gave her a job working in my record shop. Over the next few years I would continue to help my friend due to her dependency on drugs. She would later give up the use of drugs and has stayed clean to this day. Within the last few years, as recently as 1996, she worked for me off and on as a housekeeper while working full-time for Lutz Research in downtown San Diego. Later on she would go to work for my oldest brother, Sam, as a housekeeper. As time went by we drifted apart as friends. As of this writing I see her only occasionally when I run into her either downtown or in Hillcrest waiting for a bus.

During my six-month stay with Miss Duchess I hustled the streets of downtown San Diego. I would make money and I would save my money. Eventually, I had enough money to get my own place. Also during this time, I met a young man in the Navy named Earl Coins and we started a relationship. He would give me money and I would pay all the bills. This relationship lasted for about a year. One day he came to me and said he was being discharged from the Navy and that he was going back to Cleveland, Ohio, to be with his family. That was the last time I saw him. I continued to make money and meet other sailors. I also continued my run-in with the law. Eventually I ended up back in jail again.

I met Miss Bert through Miss Frances. I was at the Crossroads and still underage but I managed to pass for 21 by dressing in women's clothes. Miss Bert came into the Club one night with Miss Peaches and Miss June. Miss Frances introduced us. Miss Bert appeared to be in her early 20's and not very friendly. Later on, we would become very competitive. We were always vying for the same men or in competition to be Miss Black San Diego. She won the first two events we appeared in together but on the third one, I won. That particular night I could never forget. When I was announced the winner, Miss Bert, because she was the previous winner, it was her duty to crown the new winner. As I sat in the winning chair with cameras flashing all around me, Miss Bert took the crown, walked up to me and then turned and put the crown on the second runner up. I was so embarrassed but I held my cool and was very gracious about the whole ordeal. The person she put the crown on then came forward and placed the crown on my head. I never forgave Miss Bert for what she did that night and when she died many years Later of a massive stroke, I refused to go to her funeral. She was jealous of me because she did not have the personality or charisma I had.

Of all the drag queens during the early 60's I really admired and knew was my friend, Miss Peaches. She would always compliment me on how I looked and how I carried myself. She would always tell others how she admired me. During these years between 1960 and 1964, I made a great deal of money as a prostitute. Prior to 1962 I would go in to all the nightclubs in downtown San Diego and didn't have to show any identification even though I was still underage. There was still many times when Peaches and I were sitting at the bar at the Crossroads, The Zebra Club or the Spanish Village when vice came in. One of them was Johnny Williams, who is still alive. He later became the first black homicide detective in San Diego. He would often see me in these clubs. He would walk up to me and warn me that there were three other vice on their way and that I had better leave because they would arrest me. He was always nice to me by helping me stay out of jail.

Throughout the last forty years Miss Peaches and I remained close and loyal friends. Miss Peaches lived down the street about a quarter of a mile from my mother's house on Roswell Street. She had served in the navy for 22 years and worked as a cook for the last 10 years. When she was discharged from the Navy in the early 70's, she purchased a home in Emerald Hills. For years when I would stop in and visit my mother I would stop by and visit her. The last time I saw her, she was in a wheelchair and she was having a lot of health problems. But she still had that smile in her eyes and the joy was always there when she saw me. She would often tell people - friends and strangers about me. She would tell them that Princess Charmagne was the person who started it all in San Diego (the gay movement). Sometimes she would praise me so much that I found myself totally embarrassed. One day in February of 2005, I stopped by her home to visit with her. A young man met me at the door and told me Miss Peaches had passed away on December 7, 2004. I hadn't heard anything about it.

During my life as Princess Charmagne I would appear at different nightclubs as a female impersonator. Billed as "The Ebony Brigit Bardot" from Savannah, Georgia. Wearing a blonde wig was one of my trademarks. I appeared at The Blue Note, The Crossroad, The Elk's Club and The Convoy Club across the border in Tijuana. I became quite famous as Princess Charmagne during these female impersonator escapades. In 1962, the Elk's Club named me Miss Black Gay San Diego. A short time later, some friends of mine and I, including Sabrina Rubalcaba, Francine Francois and June attended a concert at the foot of Market St. The main attraction was Little Richard. I would never go to a concert unless I could be in the front row or had the best seats. We noticed Little Richard watching us as we carried on in the front row. Just before the concert was over we got an invitation from Little Richard to meet him in his dressing room after the show. When the show was over we were escorted backstage to the dressing room where we were introduced to Little Richard and had scotch on the rocks with him. I noticed that Little Richard was wearing tons of makeup and his hair was done professionally. He was quite the professional drag queen. I was very happy that I had met him. I would follow his career for many years and would often wonder why he never got the credit he was justly due as a singer. He was instrumental in jump-starting the career of some of the greatest singers, including The Beatles. Later on I would have the opportunity to meet Sir Lady Java, who was a nationally known drag queen. She had appeared in some of the best Hollywood cabarets, nightclubs and had been featured in Ebony and Jet Magazines.

One night while working the clubs, I met this black sailor. He was young and very handsome and seemed quite interested in me. I wasn't looking for a companion, lover or close friend at the time, but this guy was quite remarkable, and I found myself attracted to him physically. I ended up taking him home that night and thus began a relationship that became an unforgettable chapter in my life. After several months into our relationship the Navy notified him that he was being shipped overseas for duty. I was to wait for his return. He had become so attached to me that I did not realize how emotionally involved he was. I had noticed on several occasions, however, that he showed extreme jealousy when he saw me talking to other men. It never crossed my mind that he had fallen in love with me.

After he left, I continued my nightlife and having fun with other men. I would write him and he would write me and send me gifts from Germany, Switzerland and France. A drag queen named Miss Diamond came to San Diego from Los Angeles to stay with me for a while. She also was a prostitute. One night we were out working the streets when I picked up a date and took him to a motel room down town that Miss Diamond and I shared. I was there in the room with this sailor when there was a knock on the door. Before I could answer, Miss Diamond opened the door and came in. Behind her was my friend in the Navy. When he saw me in bed with the sailor, he was very upset and angry. He pushed Miss Diamond to the side and pulled out a gun. The sailor jumped out of bed and went through the glass window with no clothes on. I just lay there and looked at my friend. Then all of a sudden, I heard gunshots and he was firing the gun at me. He fired at me five times at close range and all five bullets missed me. I immediately jumped out of the bed and ran out the door naked. I ran across the street and into another hotel. One of the night attendants there knew me. He gave me a towel to wrap around myself. I left there and found myself on Market Street. I stopped a police officer and told him what happened. By that time, there were police all over the place. They took me to the city jail to make a report and to give a description of my friend. They arrested my friend that night. The next day they called me to come down to the police station and asked me if I would file charges against him. I refused so they released him. Three days later, I ran into him at another nightclub. We sat and talked and I forgave him. We remained friends, but never did we have a relationship again. Later, Miss Diamond would be sentenced to life in prison for robbery and cutting off the penis of a young sailor in Tulare, California.

CHAPTER THREE

One evening while I was getting dressed to appear at a nightclub as a female impersonator, I received a phone call from my mother saying that she needed to see me as soon as possible. I finished applying my makeup and put on my black cocktail dress, my golden mesh stockings and gold high heels. My chauffeur was waiting for me at the entrance of the apartment complex in a black limousine. I instructed the chauffer to take me to my mother's home in Emerald Hills.

When we arrived at my mother's home in Emerald Hills, my mother met me at the door. I knew right away something was wrong. She was crying and two of my youngest brothers, Carl and Glen, were on each side of her crying, too. She explained to me, while choking back tears, that my stepfather, Bill Green, was stranded in Las Vegas and he had lost all the money the family had to pay bills the following month, including the house note. The house note was $650. I gave my mother a check for $1300. She told me there was no food in the house so I instructed my chauffeur to drive me to the nearest grocery store where I bought approximately $200 worth of food. My brothers, Carl and Glen, were quite young at the time. Carl being the oldest was perhaps seven years old and Glen, about five. I don't think they realized who I was because they had never seen me in women's clothes before. Years later I would tell them about this event and why I came to the house dressed in female clothes. I guess at the time that this all unfolded I concluded that they were too young to understand why their oldest brother was wearing women's clothes.

When Bill returned back from Las Vegas he called me and said he wanted to talk to me. I went up to the house in Emerald Hills and I talked to Bill and my mother. Bill thanked me for what I had done. He said that if I wanted him to, he would put my name on the house deed. At that time, I told him and my mother that I did not want my name on the deed. That if anything should happen to them, I would rather the house go to my youngest brothers.

Between 1960 and 1964, I was arrested hundreds of times, 52 times in one year alone. I was arrested for burglary, disorderly conduct, grand theft, masquerading, failure to register as a sex offender, pimping and soliciting, possession of a switchblade knife, resisting arrest and finally, the sale of marijuana.

One night while I was walking down Market Street, three narcotic detectives picked me up. They asked me to get in the car. I asked them if I was under arrest. They said no. I refused to get in the car. As I started to walk away, two of them grabbed me and pushed me in the back seat of their unmarked car. They began to ask me questions about a friend of mine we called "Big Money". He was supposed to be a dope dealer. By being my friend they wanted to use me to set him up. I refused. Then they started beating on me and threatening me at the same time. They told me if I didn't cooperate with them they would get me. Then they let me go.

Another night I was having coffee at Prixie Coffee Shop with some friends around two o'clock in the morning, when a friend of mine, who was in the Navy and was dressed in his Navy white uniform, came to the door. I got up and went to see what he wanted. I was standing inside the doorway talking to him when a police car came by and saw me talking. They jumped out of the car, grabbed the sailor and asked me to step outside. I asked them if I was under arrest. They said no, but we want you to step outside. I refused. As I turned to go back inside, one of the police grabbed me from behind. My wig came off; I turned around and started fighting with the police officer.

We ended up fighting inside the coffee shop. We broke one section of the counter from its position and I eventually got the police officer on to the floor. I had him pinned down with my back to the front door. I managed to get his gun out of his holster. I had the gun pointed at him. I remember I felt like I had lost my mind at the time. I don't know if I was going to shoot him or not. I was completely out of my mind. Before I did anything, I was caught from behind by several police officers and they pulled me out the door. They put handcuffs on me and put me in the police car. I was taken to the police station on Market Street. My hands were handcuffed behind me. When we arrived at the police station I was pulled from the back seat of the police car. My face fell flat on the brick surface of the courtyard. The fall broke open my forehead. There was blood everywhere. Still bleeding, they took me in the station and fingerprinted me. They then threw me into a cell without giving me any treatment for my injuries. Finally, I was allowed to make a phone call. I called my attorney, J. Perry Langford. He came to the police station immediately and saw the condition of my face. He explained to me that he would call the FBI the next day and have them come down and take some pictures.

The next day, two FBI agents came to the Police Department and took several pictures and a statement from me. That evening I was released on bail. Two weeks later, I went to court for resisting arrest. I appeared in the courtroom of Judge Madge Bradley. The judge asked me "How do you plead?" I said, "Not guilty". I explained to her what had happened. She asked the arresting officer what was the probable cause of them stopping me in the first place. He said that I was soliciting a Sailor. She asked him where I (the defendant) had been standing? The officer said I was standing in the doorway. She asked him if I was outside or inside the coffee shop? The officer said I was standing inside the coffee shop, in the doorway. She asked if anyone in the coffee shop had called saying I was causing a disturbance? He said no. She asked what was the probable cause? He stated that there was a robbery two hours before, and he was investigating the robbery. Then she asked if I fit the description of the robber. He said no. Then she said, "I see no reason why you were stopping the defendant; because he was talking to a sailor? He was clearly not outside of the coffee shop. No one in the coffee shop called the police; therefore you had no probable cause to stop him. Case dismissed!" The cops? Oh, they were mad! They were mad and they were out to get me from that time on.

Also between 1960 and 1964, I was living in San Diego as well as in Los Angeles. I had an apartment in Los Angeles in the downtown area at the Carver Hotel. But my primary residence was still in San Diego. I would go to Los Angeles mainly on weekends. I had a boyfriend up there. His name was Ronald Polk. We used to hang out at the Cooper Donut Shop and at the Waldorf Astoria. One weekend while I was there, I decided to return to San Diego early. I had left the apartment that I shared with Ronald and caught the bus back to San Diego.

Three days later a detective came to my house and arrested me on a warrant for first-degree murder! Then, detectives informed me that Ronald Polk, Miss Diamond, her boyfriend and I picked up a young sailor in Tulare County, just north of Los Angeles. We robbed him, killed him and cut his penis off. I was told that Miss Diamond was stopped in downtown Los Angeles the next day and that she was carrying the penis in her purse. I told them that I was not with them. Then they asked me if I had an alibi. I said yes. I told them I did not go with my friends that morning; that I caught a bus back to San Diego and I have the bus ticket to prove it. They checked the alibi and verified that I was on the bus and actually in San Diego when the murder took place. They asked me if I knew Ronald Polk? I said yes, we live together, but I had no knowledge of what took place. They had no choice but to release me. Later, I found out that Ronald Polk, Miss Diamond and her friend were charged with first-degree murder. They were found guilty, sent to prison and sentenced to life without parole.

Los Angeles was a vast landscape of neon lights and asphalt streets. From downtown to the San Fernando Valley, dotted against the background were small shops, large hotels, bustling nightclubs and coffee shops. In the midst of downtown wedged between the Waldorf Astoria and a nondescript parking lot was Cooper Donut Shop. This was the place where we all hung out; hustlers, gay boys, drag queens and misfits. Here I met many of my friends: China Doll, Miss Diamond and later, Christina. We would meet here, have coffee and pick up tricks. There were times we went on dates together.

China Doll was a very beautiful Chinese drag queen. We were picked up one night on Sixth and Broadway by a long black chauffeured limousine. The chauffeur asked us if we were interested in making a couple hundred dollars a piece. We hopped into the back seat of the limousine and headed north toward North Hollywood. We ended up in Beverly Hills at a huge brownstone mansion, framed by a large gated iron fence. We were led into a small room with a large red curtain facing us. Suddenly the curtain parted and we both screamed at the top of our lungs! In front of us was a white casket trimmed in gold. Lying inside the casket was an elderly man dressed in a black suit with a large rose in his lapel. The curtain closed as quickly as it had opened. We were led out of the mansion and into the waiting limousine. We were each given $200 in cash by the chauffeur who explained to us what had just taken place. He said that the man we saw in the casket is a well known Hollywood producer who gets his rocks off by laying in a casket and hearing the screaming voices of females. So the man we saw in the casket wasn't dead! But little did he know that we were not females!

Two hundred dollars was a lot of money to make on a single date in those days and the more money you made the more respect you received from your peers. China Doll and I became "cause celeb" among our friends. We had many wonderful times together and made a lot of money between us. China Doll would be dressed in short mini skirts and low cut blouses or with leather pants with matching top. Her hair was always well groomed. It was black and hung below her waist. She would carry a long black Japanese cigarette holder with a gold tip. I always wore mini skirts and matching blouses with gold or silver mesh stockings with extremely high heels. We were a sight to see coming down Broadway.

There were two cops in Los Angeles named Church and Miller who hated queers, especially drag queens. When they were on the beat, we would warn each other as to their whereabouts. Twice Church and Miller arrested me for masquerading.

I spent some time in jail in Los Angeles and each time I was released, I would always return to San Diego. Even though Los Angeles was much more exciting than San Diego, I spent most of my time in San Diego. Hollywood was very exciting, especially at night. People would be everywhere on Hollywood Boulevard and Vine. You could see a man wearing a leopard skin outfit with a boa constrictor wrapped around his neck. Another man might be wearing a L'il Abner outfit and walking a huge lion on a leash, a drag queen dressed like Marilyn Monroe in the Seven Year Itch, or two guys dressed like Laurel and Hardy. Young and old were indulging in their fantasies and their dreams. Here I could make believe without being harassed or intimidated by the police. Hollywood was like a no man's land -- a dead zone. Police did not mess with you unless you were flagrantly breaking the law. You could indulge in your lifestyle and feel free to express yourself. You felt safe from those holier than thou do-gooders who believed that they were the true believers and had the right to make laws that suited their lifestyle while denying others theirs.

Malibu lies west of Los Angeles with its pristine beaches and beautiful homes. I had met an ex-priest who had become an artist. He had a beautiful home on Malibu Beach. I stayed with him off and on for the next two years. One day while we were sitting on his patio we watched a film crew making a film and was later told that they were making a movie about The Righteous Brothers. So for the next several days we watched the filming of this new movie.

One night my friend the ex-priest, took me to a unique restaurant located up in the Topanga Canyon above Pepperdine College. He told me before I got there that he had a surprise for me. As we were sitting at our table eating dinner, it was late at night; the waiters came into the dining room and pulled back large folded curtains exposing a huge picture window. Then we heard a door open. One of the busboys went outside in front of the window and placed several vats of food. He left them there. Then they went back into the restaurant. Within a few minutes there were some huge scary looking coyotes that came up to the window where we were eating and also began to eat. It was an amazing site to watch them eating on the outside while we were eating on the inside. This was the unique feature of this restaurant.

While I was staying with my friend in Malibu, I had an opportunity to visit the J. Paul Getty Art Museum, which sat on a hill above my friend's home. I was fascinated the first time I visited the museum due to my art experience as a child growing up in the south. I have always been interested in art. But what I witnessed at the J. Paul Getty Museum was really remarkable. I was in awe of the paintings and sculpture by some of the greatest artists in the world. When we got ready to leave I couldn't seem to pull myself away from all the beauty that surrounded me. I will never forget this experience.

One day while walking down the street in San Fernando Valley, a pink Cadillac convertible pulled up beside me. The driver was totally naked and had one hand on the steering wheel and the other between his legs. He was playing with himself. He asked me how I would like to make a few dollars. I asked how much, all the while wondering what type of fetish would turn him on. Three hundred dollars, he said. I got into the car and he pulled away from the curb driving very slowly. He had a nice muscular body like a weightlifter. He told me he wanted me to take my hands and massage his arms, back and legs. I massaged him for about five minutes as he masturbated. After he had reached a climax, he pulled to the curb and gave me $300 in cash. I got out of the car and kept on walking.

In Los Angeles and especially around Hollywood, there are some strange and weird people with some unusual ways of getting their pleasure. They also had no problem spending large sums of money to fulfill these fantasies. Being young, wild and eager to satisfy my own fantasies, I had no problem helping others to attain their pleasure, and, to top it off, I was compensated handsomely for my service.

But sometimes I would run into a situation where I had to draw the line. Once, I was on a date at a home in Panorama City with a middle-aged man. He asked me to take my clothes off. While I was taking my clothes off he began to take his off. As we stood there, both naked, he asked me if I would mind if he tied me up to a chair. I looked at him strangely and said yes, I would mind! I guess he realized I was serious, so he changed the subject. Then he took a basket of apples and handed them to me. He explained that he was going to bend over and that he wanted me to throw the apples at his buttocks as hard as I could. This I had no problem with, so long as he was not going to throw apples at me, or try to tie me up in a chair. After a few minutes he reached a climax and I left.

Another time, while having coffee at Cooper's Donut Shop, a guy came up to me, very nicely dressed, and asked me if I wanted to make some money. I said yes. We got in his car and drove to North Hollywood and went into his home. He said I will pay you a couple hundred dollars and the only thing you have to do is urinate in my mouth. I did!

Now as I look back over these strange experiences, I have come to believe that when it comes to sexuality, people have some strange and unusual ways of expressing themselves.

When I first heard of Christine Jorgenson, I was in Los Angeles. I picked up a newspaper one day and read about an ex-marine who had had a sex change. One of the first sex changes in America! She had changed her name from Carl to Christine Jorgenson. One night while Miss Diamond, China Doll and I were having coffee at the Golden Cup Coffee Shop on Hollywood and Vine, someone pointed out to us that Miss Jorgenson was seated at a table just to the right of us. I went over and spoke a few words with her.

I congratulated her on her bravery in undertaking such a major change in her life. She was of stocky build and was matronly. Her appearance, however, was very feminine, including her voice. One would have never guessed that she had ever been a man. She was friendly and seemed to be very happy. She was taking female hormones to give her breasts; they weren't doing many implants in the 60's. She was very attractive as a woman but not beautiful. I don't think she was ever a prostitute. But for an ex-marine to get a sex change was big news in America.

On November 22, 1963, I was asleep in my bed at my apartment at 16th and L Streets. I had been up all night the night before. There was a knock on my door. I glanced at the clock on my dresser and it was early in the afternoon. Then I heard this voice saying, "Charmagne, Charmagne, wake up!" I went to the door, opened it and my friend Miss Frances was standing there. She asked, "Have you heard the news"? I said, "What news? I've been sleeping all morning. You know me, being out all night I sleep most of the day." She said, "Turn the television on". She came into the apartment, we went into the living room, and I turned on the television.

I was stunned by what I heard. President Kennedy had been assassinated in Dallas, Texas. I couldn't believe it. I was totally devastated! It was like someone had taken a knife and cut my heart out. This was a man that I admired. A man I thought would change the world. A man whom I thought would make things right for all people. I began to look back into my own life, my past. I tried to understand why so many things seemed to happen to me. I tried to understand the gravity of what had happened with President Kennedy's assassination. And I grew depressed. I began to doubt God and believe that there was no justice, no justice whatsoever. Why must I go on? Why must I live? Although my life continued to be exciting filled with young sailors, pretty drag queens, pimps, whores and the ever-endless harassment from the law. However, there were times I was so depressed that I wanted to end my life. I had begun to realize that my whole world was a web of fantasies and a mirage of illusions that I had created for myself that was destroying my inner soul. And the reality of my existence had no meaning. I was not only deceiving myself but also all those people around me. I tried many times to escape from reality by living in a world of make-believe and false dreams. I, therefore, made several attempts to end my life.

One attempt I made on my life was when I was home alone. It was right after the assassination of President Kennedy. I seemed to have everything but the only thing that was missing was love. I wanted so desperately to be loved and accepted as a person. I decided to end my life in style. I prepared my bed and began to dress myself in my best clothes, carefully applying my makeup, placing a golden choker around my neck with matching gold earrings. I closed all the windows and doors and turned on all the gas in the apartment. I lay down on my bed with my arms beside me. Then I closed my eyes. When I opened my eyes again, I found myself in a strange room, a strange padded room. There was a nurse standing by my bed and she explained to me that I had been admitted to the county health department after attempting to commit suicide. I later found out that a friend of mine who lived two doors down from me had smelled the gas coming from my apartment and called the police. I was told they broke down my door, found me unconscious and my apartment filled with gas. They then rushed me to the hospital. I was discharged from the county hospital several weeks later and I returned to my make-believe world and continued to prostitute.

My endless confrontations with the San Diego Police Department were making it hard for me to believe in freedom, justice and equality. There were many times when they were physically abusive. Other times they escorted me to the train station, purchased a ticket, and told me to leave town. I refused to give in to their bullying and I was determined to fight for what I believed. I did not feel that wearing women's clothes was illegal and that I should be able to dress as a woman if I chose.

The mere thought of someone telling me how to dress was very disturbing. I felt I had a right to live my life as I please. I was very well aware of my rights as a citizen and there was no way that I was going to allow the police to violate those rights guaranteed by the United States Constitution.

I found myself alone in my efforts to insure the right of an individual to wear what they choose without being systematically prosecuted. Others like myself during this time were either in the closet or too afraid of the police to stand up and be counted. I truly believe to this day that I was the first gay activist in America and especially in California. (In California at the time, there was a law against "masquerading" in effect.) Some may argue that "Stonewall", which happened in New York City, was the beginning of the gay movement. But it must be pointed out that Stonewall happened in the late 60's, long after a decision made by a Judge Bradley in 1963, in California. Stonewall was a name of a nightclub in New York City where the gays hung out. The police broke in and were going to arrest them for something, perhaps for cross-dressing and a fight broke out. A lot of people went to jail, but it was later found there was no cause to make the arrest. Stonewall is still celebrated today as the beginning of the gay movement. I know for a fact that the decision handed down by Judge Madge Bradley in 1963, before Stonewall, first set the stage for the gay movement and made it unconstitutional for the police to arrest a man for masquerading as a woman.

One night, while going from bar to bar, I picked up a businessman at The Crossroads. He had quite a bit of money on him and he was spending a lot of it on me, buying drinks. Soon he decided he wanted to go to Tijuana and party. We arrived in Tijuana late that night. One of our first stops was the Convoy Club. Then we ended up at the Blue Note. He was getting very drunk, so I decided that we must go back to the States. We were standing outside waiting for a taxi when he walked to the corner and began to take a leak behind a building. The Police came and arrested him. I decided to catch a taxi and go back. I had to get out of there. I was still waiting on the corner for a taxi when a car pulled up with two Mexican boys in it.

I did not realize there were four in the car. I could see only two (I was a little intoxicated myself). They asked me where I was going. I said I wanted to go to the Border. They offered to give me a ride. I got into the car. Instead of taking me to the Border, they took me South of Tijuana. I soon realized that my life was in danger. I had on some very expensive jewelry and I was well dressed. So no doubt they thought I had money on me as well. When we got outside Tijuana, I asked them where they were taking me. One of them pulled out a knife and threatened me. I told them I did not have much money on me. I knew I had to react and think of something very quick because I had known other people who had been in this same situation who ended up dead. So I told them that my father was a very wealthy American; that he owned several nightclubs and that whatever amount of money they wanted, I would be willing to get it if they would take me back to Tijuana so I could make a phone call. But before they took me back to TJ, all four of them raped me. Even after they found out I was not a woman. There was one particular young Mexican boy. I remember when he pulled his penis out that he had sores around it. I am quite sure that he had some type of sexually transmitted disease. But at the moment, that wasn't important because my life was at stake! When we got back to Tijuana, we stopped at an intersection and I got the opportunity to open the door and jump out of the car. I ran! Finally, I got back to the Border and took a taxi home. They had taken everything.

Three weeks later, I began to feel pains around my scrotum area; excruciating pains. Then I noticed little sores starting to appear around my scrotum and rectum. A few days later, I discovered that these sores had begun to fester with white puss. I went to the doctor. The doctor examined me, did some tests and gave me a penicillin shot. He told me to come back in three days. When I went back, he had the test results that indicated I had some type of venereal disease, but he didn't know what it was. He told me it was a very rare type of disease that was also rare to the United States. He put me on a treatment of penicillin. After several weeks, I didn't seem to be any better. I was constantly walking in pain nearly every day, but continued with my treatment. I also continued with my nightlife, but was very cautious not to have sexual intercourse. I limited myself to oral sex.

During this period, as I was sitting at the bar at the Kiddeo #I Club, a friend of mine, named Puppet, (we both had attended San Diego High together), came in with a young Mexican dude. He walked up to me and asked me if I had any marijuana? I replied that I didn't. He asked me if I could get some for him. I said I might be able to. He told me that he and his friend were going to a party and they wanted to get loaded before they got there. He said he would appreciate it if I could get some (marijuana) for him. I told him to wait at the club and I would go around to the Zebra Club and see if "Money" was there (he sells marijuana and dope, etc.). If he had any I would come back and let him know. I walked around to the Zebra Club. Money was there. I asked him if he had any marijuana. He said he had a very small amount in a cellophane bag that he would let me have for $5. I went back around and told Puppet. He gave me $5. I went back to the Zebra Club and purchased the marijuana, came back and gave it to Puppet. He and his friend then left the club.

Three months later, I was at my apartment sleeping early in the morning when there was a loud bang on my front door. I heard, "Police, Police, open up!" Before I could open the door, they broke the door down. They pounced on me, put handcuffs on and told me I was under arrest on a secret indictment for one count of sales of marijuana. I soon realized that the police had set me up with my friend, Puppet. They had finally made good on their threat that they would get me and send me to prison. I was in jail for several weeks before my trial. During this period, my infectious condition worsened. The day of my trial I was brought into the courtroom in a wheelchair with clear plastic visqueen wrapped around me. The disease I had contracted in Mexico had spread over most of my scrotum and the open sores had become worse. The visqueen was a safety precaution. The court found me guilty and sentenced me to five years to life. The next day, I was taken from the San Diego County Jail directly to Chino Prison and hospitalized in the hospital ward.

Several days later, the doctor came in and told me that I would be going in for surgery. They were going to cut all around my scrotum area and place drainage, so that all the infection I had would drain out. I would be on antibiotics for several weeks. After surgery, Dr. William Frankborne, came to my room and told me that if I hadn't come to prison when I did and had the surgery, that I would probably have been dead in two or three weeks. He said I was lucky that I had been sent to prison. They never knew what the disease was, but labeled it lympho granuloma venereal. It continues to be a constant problem for me to this day and I often have to seek medical treatment for it. I truly believe that all the tests they did on me for HIV later that were positive, were part and parcel of this particular disease.

During my stay in the hospital while in prison, I met a young man who was my nurse. He would come into my room several times during his shift. He would bathe me and turn me every two hours. Turning me because I was too weak to move myself. He would spend time talking to me and understood the nature of my medical condition, in which he took great interest. Before I left the hospital we had become very close friends. Our relationship continued after I left the hospital and went into the main population of the prison. Our relationship was short-lived. Soon I was transferred out of Chino Prison to Vacaville Medical Facility.

Little Black Book

During my escapades as Princess Charmagne, between 1960 to 1964, I kept a small black address book. There were names, addresses and telephone numbers of most of my clients and associates, including police officers, businessmen, political figures and other prominent members of San Diego and Los Angeles society. When I was arrested in 1964 for the sale of marijuana, this little black book contained over 100 names of individuals, with whom I either had an intimate relationship or personal business dealings. After my arrest, I had a trusted friend go to my apartment to collect my personal property and place it in storage for me. I asked him to look for this book and he informed me that it was not among any of my property. I kept this little black book in a very special place, inside a hand-carved wooden box. When he told me it was not in this box, I knew without a doubt that the police had seized it. Later, when I asked the officers about it, they were unaware of any such book. The disappearance of this book was a relief to many, including some members of the San Diego Police Department.

Years later, doing time at Vacaville Medical Facility, I was informed by a reliable source that the officers who arrested me, seized the little black book by orders of higher-ups in the police department. To this day, I have had dreams and visions of this little black book, with all those names, addresses and phone numbers dancing in my head. I too, find a sense of relief that I didn't have to expose those individuals listed in my book.

CHAPTER FOUR

This was my first time in prison. I was extremely nervous and scared because I had heard so much about prison life. When I arrived in Vacaville in 1964, I discovered that my brother, Sam, was there also! And, in the first few weeks I also discovered that my oldest brother was also a queen! I always had my suspicions about his sexuality, but due to the fact we were never close as kids, I never knew precisely that he was a homosexual.

He was well known at Vacaville. He had some type of racket going on. He was bribing some of the guards and had a group of prisoners with him wherever he went in prison. I noticed that there were other prisoners at Vacaville that were afraid of him. I remember a couple of incidents where inmates were killed while in their cells and my brother, Sam, was questioned about it. One time he was arrested and taken to isolation after another inmate was killed. A few days later he was released from isolation back to the mainline. For the first time since we were kids he seemed to realize that I did exist, and that we were brothers. I knew this because during my stay at Vacaville, he made sure that I was safe and if I had any trouble with anyone, he was there to take care of the matter. It did not take me long, however, before I had gained some type of influence myself in the prison setting with other prisoners. I remember one time a friend of mine came to me and told me that there were a couple guys who wanted to set my brother up to be killed. They believed he had too much power. I talked to some of my friends and we met with these guys. I managed to squash whatever plot they had conceived to get rid of my brother by paying them off with a large amount of cigarettes. I never told my brother that I intervened in a situation that perhaps saved his life. Even as of this writing he does not know.

After about two years on the mainline, my brother was transferred to another institution while I remained at Vacaville. During my last year there, I made some important contacts with other members of prison gangs and also had a good relationship with some of the corrupt guards who worked there. In 1967, I was paroled back to San Diego, California.

After many years of analyzing my past and researching my soul I have come to the conclusion that within me are two individuals, Princess Charmagne and David Brown. I have one body with two souls, each as different as night and day. Princess Charmagne is the realist, an extrovert and a beautiful soul reaching out always to help others. She believes that what happens, happens for the best and one must keep looking ahead regardless of how bad a situation might appear to be. When I was dressed as Princess Charmagne I felt real; like this was the real me.

I felt that I was a woman trapped in a man's body and when I was Princess Charmagne, I fulfilled all the desires that was truly me and that was as a woman. She made me feel wonderful, empowered, and in control of things around me.

Princess Charmagne was also known as La Princess and the Lady with the Champagne Taste. However, there was another person that was vying for control of my body, but La Princess maintained her grip and continued her complete control. Dressed in her finest attire with a blonde wig framing her feminine face with large hazel eyes and full sensual lips left no doubt when you heard her feminine and sexy voice, that she was indeed a woman. Many stories about her looks and feminine ways can attest to this. For five years the Princess reigned supreme in my body shared by another soul.

It was in 1964 that she had to relinquish some of her control to this other soul. That was the year that I went to prison (Vacaville). During the next three years while serving time for the sale of marijuana, Princess Charmagne started to lose control and David Brown began to emerge. At first there was a struggle as to whom would be the dominant force in my life and in the battle of control, La Princess held her own. But, David soon began to emerge, as the dominant one to be reckoned with and in the near future would take control away from Princess. It was in the late 70's when La Princess began to lose her supreme grip and David emerged in complete control which not only changed the feminine nature of my body but the unique and sophisticated personality that once belonged to Princess Charmagne.

While in prison, of course, I couldn't dress like a woman. I could wear tight pants, shirts and wear makeup, but not high heels. That's when Princess Charmagne began to be phased out.

David Brown was just the opposite of Princess Charmagne. He began to emerge in the late 60's and took total control in the early 80's. Princess Charmagne had become a faded memory; a distant dream that once was a part of me. Perhaps she is still there inside of me waiting for another opportunity to regain her dominancy and control my body once again. David was more of an introvert and self-centered. He seemed to shy away from most people and had distrust for others, especially the police. He harbored a lot of anger because of all those years he spent behind bars shuffling from one prison to another. Those years were wasted years for crimes he did not commit. When I discovered David, I was shocked to realize that he had been there all along. I truly believe that all the trouble and abuse of prison life I had, and the political awareness that I had acquired while incarcerated, brought him out of me.

Princess Charmagne was meek, humble and good-natured and would not have been able to handle the deep-seated hatred that I had accumulated within my soul all those years. David was the only one who could avenge the wrong that had been done to me and who had the ability and intellect to exonerate my soul from those unjustifiable miscarriages of justice.

After being in Vacaville for several months, and having an affair with one particular person, I began to settle down and learn the ropes of prison life. I quickly learned that no one likes "snitches" or child molesters. But I had no problem with either of these offenses. While there I witnessed several murders committed by prisoners of other prisoners. One in particular stands out in my mind. I was on my way to the main dining room for dinner. Coming down the stairway from the third floor, there was a young man directly in front of me. As we got to the bottom of the steps on the first floor, several Mexican guys rushed into the stairway and stabbed the young man repeatedly. I stepped over the bleeding young man and continued on to the dining room. When I was approached by the prison guards and asked what I saw, I told them

I saw nothing. That was it! I saw nothing. I later found out that the young man had snitched on one of the Mexican dudes and that he died later in the hospital. He had been stabbed thirty-two times.

During my stay in prison from 1964 to 1967, I had numerous relationships with other men. In prison, when you have a relationship with a guy, you are considered a married couple. You did not cheat on that person. They didn't cheat on you. Sometimes out in the real world you would have disagreements and separate or divorce from that person and you find somebody else, which typically leads to conflicts to say the least! The person you're divorcing can get very jealous and angry and someone can even end up dead. Such was the case with a very popular drag queen. Her name was Louise Brown, she was involved with a young man who was very jealous of her, because Louise was very young, very beautiful and he could not accept the fact that he was losing this person to someone else. So he got two of his friends to lay in wait for Miss Brown as she was coming out of one of her classes on the second floor of the school building. They then stabbed her to death. Three people were involved in her murder and were arrested. It was a very shocking situation for the rest of the queens at Vacaville Medical Facility. And it was a sensational topic among the entire prison population for the next several months. The most ironic part was she was very beautiful, dark skinned black queen involved with a white man - in prison that is very unusual. Louise didn't like black guys, but you would never say that in prison. Two of the guys who murdered her were black.

While in prison from 1964 until 1967, my most memorable affair was with a young man named Willie C. Reeves. At the time I met Willie I was in relationship with another young man named Rodney. Rodney and I were having some problems and we were on the verge of breaking up. It seemed that Willie came along at the right time. He was a new inmate, very handsome and all the queens were talking about him and how sexy he looked. We met in the main library one afternoon and began to talk. The next day we went to breakfast together. It so happened that Rodney was also having breakfast in the same dining room. He appeared to be upset. Finally he came over to our table and had words with Willie. They began to argue. Finally he left and

Willie and I went back to the library. Three days later Willie and I were in the men's advisory counsel office, where I served as one of the representatives on the counsel. Rodney came in and began an argument with Willie and pulled out a shank (knife). He made an attempt to stab Willie. I stepped in between them and demanded that Rodney give me the shank. Finally he handed me the shank and with tears in his eyes said that he did not want me to leave him. I looked at him and then I looked at Willie and said, "There is no reason for two grown men to be fighting over another man, so why don't you both share me?" They agreed and I left them by themselves in the office. I took the shank and got rid of it. (By the way, having a shank in my possession was a felony, so I ditched it in the big yard.) Thereafter, Willie, Rodney and I remained close friends.

I also first met Miss Lorraine at Vacaville Medical Facility during my first incarceration. Miss Lorraine was younger than I and very pretty. He looked, walked and acted like a girl. We soon became bitter rivals. There were other queens there whose femininity and beauty far exceeded Miss Lorraine and mine. I had a quality that was more unique than all the rest. I had a charisma that seemed to captivate the eyes of the men around me. Miss Lorraine's beauty was only evidenced from the outside. On the inside his soul was filled with jealousy and envy because of my reputation. He was always saying nasty things about me and would try to destroy my relationships with my lovers and friends. One day he approached me about something someone had told him. He heard that I had been talking about him and his old man. He cursed me and called me an old fag and over the hill. I looked him straight in the eyes and said, "Miss Thing, I might be older than you, but I sure as hell have more experience than you, and I will one day have the opportunity to dance at your funeral." Miss Lorraine was paroled before I, and he/she returned to San Diego. When I was paroled about a year later, I ran into her several times on the streets of San Diego. About a year after that, Miss Sabrina told me Miss Lorraine had passed away. He was only in his late 20's. Apparently she was a victim of drugs and alcohol that caused kidney failure. A few days later I attended his funeral at Christ Church in Logan Heights. While attending the funeral I couldn't help but think about what I said to him in prison about dancing at his funeral. I often wonder if I was somehow responsible for his death.

During my three years at Vacaville Medical Facility, I worked in the laundry for about a year and then went to work for a lieutenant in the custody office. I was a clerk responsible for typing inmate infraction reports called 115's. Every time an inmate broke the rules or committed another infraction, the investigating officer would make a crime report. The reports were brought to my desk for filing and typing before they were submitted to the program Lieutenant. On many occasions I would do favors for some of the inmates who had received these infractions by either altering the report, or causing a mistake in the report which led to the infraction, thereby getting it dismissed by the Lieutenant for whom I worked. I would receive kickbacks from these inmates in the form of cigarettes or money. While I was working in the Custody Office, I saw privileged information that was regarded highly confidential, things such as raids scheduled for certain inmates, or information regarding persons who were admitted on a sex crimes. Admittedly, I would sometimes use this information to my advantage. While working as a clerk, I was given a parole hearing after I had served three years and was given a six month parole date.

When I was released from prison in 1967, I went back home to stay with my mother in San Diego mainly because I had no other place to go. A few days after my release, Clyde invited me to a party at one of his friend's homes in Logan Heights. We went together. When we arrived, there were six or seven people already there, drinking, smoking and having fun. Just having been released from prison and my first time going out, after a few drinks I found myself drunk. I never seemed to get used to alcohol because it caused me to become intoxicated very quickly. The next thing I remember, I was in the bedroom with several people. We were all nude and indulging in a sex orgy. Then to my shock, I found my brother, Clyde, on top of me having sexual intercourse! The memory of this incident remained a vivid part of my past. Afterwards, we never spoke of the incident.

I met Gene Washington in 1967 downtown in a nightclub called The Crossroads. He was in the Navy and was stationed at the Navy Pier on

32nd and Pacific Coast Highway. He was from Denver, CO and he had only been in the Navy for two years. The night we met he went home with me and I told him all about my life.

I was working and had a job at a local construction company at the time I met him. I had an apartment on 26th and Market Street. It was a nice apartment sitting up on a hill across from a hospital. I loved it because it had large French picture windows and a huge living room. It was Victorian style. Gene spent most of his time on duty at the naval station, and when he was not at home, I would watch television or go out and visit friends.

One particular night I was lying on the sofa watching television. Gene had called me earlier and said he would not be coming in because of duty. As I was lying there, I heard a knock on the door. I got up from the sofa, answered the door, and as I opened the door, there stood a young black man with a skullcap on his head. He asked me, "Does James live here?" I answered and said; No, James lives here. Then he asked if was sure? I said yes. I heard a popping sound and then another popping sound. I felt myself falling back from the door onto the floor. As I was falling, I remember slamming the door closed. I began to feel pain in my stomach. I grabbed my stomach with my hand and the pain increased. The dress I was wearing at the time was a lavender in color and I could not see any blood, anywhere. I did not realize he shot me, but I knew I was hurt. I knew I had to get help. I reached for the telephone but could not get a dial tone. I crawled to the front door and opened it. There was no one there. I crawled down six flights of stairs to the sidewalk. Then I crawled twenty-five feet to the corner and another twenty-five feet to the manager's apartment.

When I reached the manager's apartment I was semi-conscious, but I do remember reaching for the doorbell. That's the last thing I remember until I heard sirens. Then I felt hands on me moving me. I heard voices and the next thing I remembered was a priest saying last rites over me. Someone said, take "her" to the operating room immediately! Three days later, I woke up in a hospital room with tubes everywhere. I had tubes coming out of my throat and out of the side of my body. The doctor came in later that evening and told me I was a lucky man. That if I hadn't got to the hospital when I did, I would have been dead. They said they could not remove the bullet because it was too close to my spinal cord. I found out later that the gunman was looking for someone else, and since he could not find that person, he shot me!

It was amazing to me that I had reached my manager's apartment after having been shot and bleeding internally and becoming semi-conscious between the time I left my apartment, and climbing down the stairs. That was just one version of what happened to me. Later, after I went back to prison, I was told by a reliable source that the police was behind the shooting. That's what I was told. They wanted to get rid of me because of my activism in the gay community.

Another reason was because of the assault that night in 1963 when I was standing in the doorway of the coffee shop talking to my friend when the police came by and tried to arrest me. The police never found out who did the shooting and I don't think they did much investigating. There was not a thorough investigation of the shooting. The only person aside from my friend Gene that came to visit me while I was in the hospital was my uncle, Reverend Lee Henderson. After I was released from the hospital, Gene and I moved from 26th Street closer to the Naval Base on 32nd Street. It was while at this apartment I was arrested for having allegedly kidnapped and sexually assaulted Steven Shockley.

When I was paroled from Vacaville Medical Facility in 1967, I worked as a construction worker for several contractors and during this time I met a lady. We became friends; she had a nephew named Steven Shockley. My friend told me that he was having some problems in school and hanging out downtown at gay nightclubs. She wanted to know if I could help him in some way. I remember I occasionally picked him up at his aunt's house and took him to school. I would also sometimes take him to my apartment and talk to him about getting an education. I told him that he should listen to his aunt and stay away from downtown. He appeared to understand and listen to what I was telling him. I did not consider him to be a juvenile in any way, just a little bit confused because of not having any parents, just an aunt. I could relate to him because of my own past; having a mother who didn't mother, and never knowing who my father is as if I had no parents all.

I thought at time that I was getting to know him and that he was making some progress, especially in school. Then one day I was at home when the police came by. They asked me some questions about Steve and I answered them. They told me Steve had made statements against me. He told them that I had kidnapped him and had sex with him. I told the officer that it was not true. He asked me where I was on a particular day and I told him I was at home. Did you see Shockley that day? I answered no. They placed me under arrest and took me to jail. I called my attorney, Mr. Langford, and I explained to him what had happened. I was informed by Mr. Langford that the victim, Steven Shockley, had indicated that while he was in my car I pulled a gun from underneath my clothes and threatened him. He further stated I took him to my residence and threatened him again with a shiny instrument similar to a knife or an ice pick. Steve said he was forced to remove his clothing below the waist and to lie on the bed while I forced my penis into his anus. Steve then stated that I drove him to school and threatened him not to report the incident. Steve told his aunt of the "incident" approximately five days later.

On May 30, 1968, I was found guilty of infamous crime against nature, kidnapping and assault with a deadly weapon. I was convicted on circumstantial evidence only! I was innocent! The victim, while on the witness stand, told many contradictory stories as to what had happened during the incident and was later impeached in a number of instances by the defense attorney. As of this day I declare my innocence of the charges as I stated in 1968 to the investigating officers. However, I was sent back to prison, first to Chino, then to Vacaville Medical Facility.

At the same time I was helping Steve, I was still involved with Gene Washington. We had a very good relationship. I had steady employment making good money. We had a very nice apartment. We had everything going for us. I thought at this time maybe I would make it. But when I was convicted of that crime, I was devastated! I lost everything - my apartment, my furniture, my livelihood and most of all, Gene. I never saw him again. I heard he went back to Denver. He is one person I would like to see again.

From 1968 until 1974 I was in prison. It was my second time as an inmate at Vacaville Medical Facility. I was less nervous because I knew how to survive in such a jungle. There were still people there that were there the last time I was in Vacaville. I was angry!

During my second stay at Vacaville, I was assigned to work in the hospital as an orderly due to my previous medical background. I worked on the second floor and one of my patients happened to be the famous Country and Western singer, Spade Cooley. Spade Cooley was hospitalized with a bad heart. I had to monitor him every two hours and take his vital signs. He was a very jolly person and always seemed to be happy and cracking jokes. He would tell me about some of the things that had happened in his past and some of the places he had been. But we never discussed why he was incarcerated. It was well known among the general population that he had killed his wife and then took a cigarette and burned holes all over her body.

It was one of California's most celebrated criminal cases in the 1950's. In the early 70's, Spade Cooley had a parole hearing and was given a parole date. Before he was released his doctor told him that he would not be able to give any more concerts. However, a few days after his release he was giving a concert in San Francisco and had a heart attack on stage and died! We heard the news the next day.

There were also a few other famous alumni that I had the pleasure of knowing, or who happened to be housed in Vacaville Medical Facility at the same time as I. There was Mayor Houlihan, who at that time was Mayor of Oakland, California. The most famous of all was Charles Manson. I often witnessed Manson walking down the hallway surrounded by at least four guards. When he had to go to visit someone, go to the hospital, or give interviews, the main hall was cleared of all inmates and an entourage of guards would escort him. I never got to know him personally, but I often saw him walking. He was always as weird looking as the day he was arrested. He never shaved or did anything to take care of himself. He was in complete lockup and isolated from the rest of the population.

Another famous inmate was a Hungarian doctor there who was convicted of chopping his wife's head off. I remember one time during this period an inmate had disappeared and the officials could not find him. There was no evidence that he had escaped but the next day his body was discovered in the kitchen, chopped up inside one of the big cooking vats, he was actually in the soup!

I was also very active in such inmate activities as the Black Cultural Association (BCA), the Chess Club, and the Men's Advisory Counsel. I was the founder and publisher of The Black Liberator, which was a weekly publication published by the BCA. This was a political magazine that consisted of the politically oriented writings of militant inmates. Many of the articles that were submitted to me by these militant individuals had to be edited several times by the Program Lieutenant and myself before I could publish them.

This magazine was widely read by the black prison population and by outside guests who were given issues of the publication when they came to the Friday Night meetings of the BCA. There was an approved list of people who could come in from the outside. During this time, as a member of the BCA and publisher of the black liberator, I became a good friend of Donald Defreeze and a brother named Death Row Jeff. Donald Defreeze, Death Row Jeff, another brother named Deganih and myself formed a secret organization called the Symbionese Liberation Army, better known as the SLA. This secret organization functioned under the auspices of the BCA. Due to the political nature of the SLA, it would have been outlawed by the administration of the prison if they had known of its existence. There were only a few black brothers who were members of this organization, the SLA. Because the prison administration would not allow inmates to espouse their political views, the SLA served as a conduit for these politically minded brothers. Donald Defreeze and I disagreed on the method of how to achieve a successful political struggle in this country.

He had his own methods and I had mine. Shortly after we had formed the organization, the prison officials suspected SLA activity and proceeded to break it up. Donald DeFreeze and I were transferred to Soledad State Prison. Death Row Jeff was transferred to San Quentin; Degahin was transferred to Folsom State Prison. Several other members suspected of SLA activity were transferred to other state prisons.

Donald and I were housed in different wings in the mainline population of Soledad Prison. We were able to socialize and communicate with each other after we were transferred. Before I was transferred from Vacaville to Soledad, I was taken to the custody office and told by several prison officials that they knew of my involvement and illegal activities. They were sending me to Soledad Prison so that I would get killed. That's exactly what they told me! The purpose in telling me this was because I was gay and in Soledad the mainline population was not suitable for gay people. In fact, I would be the only openly gay person probably in the history of Soledad mainline.

No one had ever been housed under these circumstances. However, my stay at Soledad Prison was without incident except for one. That one incident involved a black inmate who wanted to have sex with me against my will and it was rumored that if I didn't have sex with him that he would kill me. By this time I was in a position that I was not afraid of anyone. I had too many friends through my affiliation with the SLA who were also at Soledad. One of these individuals was head of the BGF (Black Gorilla Family), which was another illegal political organization. I went to the head of the BGF and explained my problem; that this person said he would kill me if I didn't have sex with him. He took care of the situation.

After a year on the mainline, Donald came to me one day and told me he was planning to escape. He told me how he was going to do it through the boiler room where he worked. He had arranged for some people on the outside to pick him up. He wanted to know if I wanted to go with him. I told him no, because I had just gone to my parole board hearing and they had given me a date to go home. I told him I would see him when I was released on parole. I had a six-month parole date. Donald DeFreeze escaped through the boiler room as he had planned and I was waiting to be paroled so I could join him on the streets. Approximately two weeks after he escaped, he and several members of the SLA kidnapped Patty Hearst and made headline news. I followed with interest the twists and turns of the SLA on television from inside the walls of Soledad state prison. I watched with horror as the house burned with DeFreeze and other SLA members.

CHAPTER FIVE

After being paroled from Soledad Prison in 1974, I went back to San Diego where I began to try to piece my life back together. I went back into construction work and into prostitution. While I was at Soledad I had taken some law courses and became head of the law library there. With this knowledge of law, I also did some paralegal work on the side. My prostitution brought me in conflict with the law again while still on parole. I was picked up for disorderly conduct, prostitution in 1975, and in 1976, I was picked up again for disorderly conduct and lewd acts, prostitution and resisting arrest. In 1976 again, I was picked up for petty theft and contributing to the delinquency of a minor. In 1978, prostitution again but there was never any charges brought except misdemeanors and fines. It was simply harassment. There was no prison; no parole violation. I was finally discharged from parole on December 28, 1977.

In 1976, while still on parole, I met a young man named Robert Ray Davis. When I first met Robert, it was at the San Diego County Courthouse. He was 16 years old. I was there as a paralegal consultant to another young man who was going to court. Robert approached me and wanted to know if I would assist him with his legal problem. He was facing a charge of possession of marijuana. I advised him as to what he needed to do and afterwards we became very close friends. He introduced me to his mother and stepfather who lived near my mother in Emerald Hills. His mother had told me that she wouldn't allow him to stay with her due to his drug problems. That's how he ended up staying with me. I made it clear to him that since he was only 16 years old, it would be against the law for me to have anything to do with him personally.

His mother knew he was staying with me and had approved, as long as he minded his own business, there should be no problem. In fact, during the two years he stayed with me, he went to school and got very good grades. After graduating from high school, at the age of 17, I sent him to a labor training school where he got his certificate to become a construction worker. This was at the time when I was working for the Ninteman Construction Company as a supervisor for the owner,

V. J. Ninteman. When Robert finished his labor training, I got him a job working at Ninteman Construction, too. He was being paid $9 per hour as a laborer and he was assigned to me. V. J. Ninteman and other employees assumed that Robert was my son. There was no reason for them to believe otherwise. When Robert became 18 years old, we began a personal relationship. I had had knowledge of his past escapades with friends of mine with whom he had also slept and smoked dope. We would go to his mother's house sometimes three and four times a week and visit them. He had three sisters and two brothers.

Jimmy Rutherford, was the youngest brother of Robert. My dear beloved Jimmy was a handsome and caring teenager. He spent most of his time with me and Robert when he was just 16 years old. He was always cooperative and well mannered. He was born in Little Africa (an area of San Diego) in the heart of a ghetto and never had an opportunity to enjoy the finer things of life. When I first met Robert, Jimmy would come to visit us and often spend the night. He seemed to be very happy to be around us. He was closest to his older brother, Robert and was extremely unhappy living at home with his family. He enjoyed his freedom being with us. One day he asked me if he could live with us. I told him I would ask his mother. Several days later, I was visiting the family so I asked Martha, his mother, if Jimmy could come and live with Robert and me.

It was only a year prior that I had asked her to let his brother Robert stay with me. Martha had six children; three boys and three girls. I think she was happy to have someone help her out with her kids. She was appreciative of the offer and happy that Jimmy could get away from the negative environment in which he was living. When he came to stay with us, I tried everything I could to make him happy. He was just like the son I never had, and I showered him with gifts and spending money. I paid for his education, dropped him off at school in the morning and picked him up in the evening. It wasn't unusual to see him dressed in a three piece, pinstriped suit just like mine, and walking beside me when we went out together. I would buy him expensive shirts, pants, sweaters and designer shoes, he would go on to earned the title as the "Best Dressed Little Kid in School" (informally).

There was many times when Robert and I would get into an argument because of Robert's misbehavior. Jimmy would tell Robert that he should be grateful and appreciative for all the things I did for him. Jimmy seemed to possess a knowledge and understanding of life far more mature than others his age. Indeed, he had a better understanding of life than Robert! His appreciation for the many things I did for him would always show in his eyes and I could see the joy in his smile when I gave him something he wanted. It made me feel that I was contributing to making his life better and, in turn, making me feel wonderful. I would not have done anything that might have caused him harm or bring unhappiness into his life, thus destroying this unique relationship between he and I. Jimmy was also aware of my relationship with Robert and it did not bother him. Robert and I were very discrete, we had to be, unlike the relationships he had with his girlfriends.

Later when I went to prison, Jimmy returned to stay with his mother in Little Africa. Eventually I learned he ended up with a lady named Rossgene who lived a couple of doors from his mother. Rossgene had a bad reputation. She was a skillful con artist, shoplifter and dope pusher.

All her kids had been in and out of trouble their entire lives and she had been in jail several times herself. When I was told that he was living with Rossgene, I began to worry about his welfare. But I was in prison and there was nothing I could do to help him. When I was released in 1981, I tried to get in contact with Jimmy but failed. Eventually, while in Imperial Beach, I was told by a friend of mine that Jimmy was dead. I could not believe what I had heard. My friend told me he had been killed in a shoot-out; caught between two rival gangs at Colina Park just two weeks prior! Jimmy was just an innocent bystander who happened to be in the wrong place at the wrong time. Apparently they rushed him to Paradise Hospital where he later died. He had just celebrated his 18th birthday. I was devastated by the news. For weeks I suffered emotional pain whenever I saw his pictures hanging on the wall in the living room. If only I could have been told of his death when it happened, I could have paid my last respects to a very wonderful and adoring kid whom I will always consider my son.

My relationship with Robert appeared to be parental. But, in fact, it was really a mutual and reciprocal love relationship. The relationship went well for the next several months. It was Robert's drug problem that was the only thing that seemed to cause problems in our relationship. He would work hard, help me pay bills, but he was still running around with his friends smoked pot. I would approach him about the situation but to no avail. I found out he had progressed to using cocaine, which he could not afford continually as a habit. I was trying to save money to buy a home and found myself spending more money on him and his drug problem. His infidelity became such a problem for me, that I too became unfaithful.

In one particular instance, I picked up a girl and brought her to our apartment. As we walked into the living room she had a certain surprised look on her face. I asked her what was wrong. She told me that she been to my apartment before, in fact it was just a few days ago. With whom I asked? She said don't you have a friend named Robert? Yes, he's my lover I replied. He brought me here and tried to have sex with me, but I wouldn't let him she said.

When Robert came home that night, I asked him about it. One thing led to another and we ended up in a physical fight. I must have got the worst of it, because he managed to tie my hands behind me (I must have been unconscious). The next thing I knew he placed some plastic material over my face and began to and suffocate me. He was trying to kill me! He suddenly realized what he was doing. He slowly took the plastic off my face and untied me. After letting me loose, He sat on the bed, hunched over, holding his head in his hands. I stood there looking at him and realized he was in a drugged induced state. Ironically, from this incident he realized being on drugs caused him to do things that he might later regret. On the other hand, for me this incident seemed to bring us a bit closer, or so I thought. When we went to visit his family, we appeared to be happy and free of any problems. However, his mother knew something was wrong. She confronted me about it one day and so I told her. She also knew that we were lovers. After learning about our relationship and his drug problem, she talked to Robert, telling him he should stop using drugs and stop treating me the way he was treating me, because I had done more for him than anybody ever had. That he should appreciate it. His mother, his sisters and brothers are still my friends. And I still visit them. I would discover later he continued to use drugs and he continued to run around and cheat as before. I decided to simply overlooked his behavior.

One day, Robert got so strung out on drugs that I had to shoot at him. The bullet missed him and went into the wall. He fled out the front door. A few days later I found out that he had drawn most of the money out of our account and he had stolen some jewelry that I had at the house. He took it with him. He had disappeared; no one knew where he was. I took my gun one day and went looking for him. I looked for him for the next two or three weeks but couldn't find him. One day, while shopping at Big Bear's Market on Federal Boulevard, I saw him going through the line. I went outside the store, got my gun out of the car and when he came out of the store I approached him. He had his back to me so I pointed my finger in his back as I walked up to him. He turned around facing me and I put the gun in his chest. He threw up his hands. I pulled the trigger and the gun misfired. It clicked but it didn't fire. When he heard that click, he ran. I ran after him at the same time pulling the clip out of the gun and inserting another clip. This time the gun did not misfire and I started shooting at him.

People in the parking lot of the grocery store started ducking under their cars trying to get out of the way and I kept chasing him across the bridge over Interstate 94 on Euclid Avenue, just two blocks from his mother's house. He ran into the house and I stopped. I walked back to my car and as I was walking back across the bridge toward the grocery store there were police cars with sirens blaring everywhere. They passed right by me. By this time I realized they knew what had happened and were probably looking for me. So I took the gun and threw it over the bridge. It landed on the embankment of the 94 Freeway. I walked back to my car without being stopped, got in and drove off. I was still angry, I was frustrated, I was mad. I was mad as hell. When I caught up with him I was going to kill him, get in my car, drive to Mexico, buy some Seconals and some whiskey, get a hotel room and commit suicide. Instead, since I didn't have a gun, I went to Mexico anyway, where I purchased another gun and came back to the States.

Somehow, I can't specifically remember how, but I knew he was going to be at a certain place at a certain time that weekend. The event was a Richard Pryor concert. Someone had told me that he had purchased tickets to the concert. So I posted myself outside the concert hall, with the new gun I had purchased. Unbeknownst to me, Richard Pryor had appeared in Los Angeles just prior to arriving in San Diego and someone had made an attempt on his life. So the security guard at the concert that night was checking everyone going through the entrance. I finally saw Robert appear in the crowd of people going in. I moved in behind him several feet, but there were so many people I was afraid I would hit someone. So I decided to follow him into the concert hall. I had a long burgundy leather coat on. It almost touched the ground. I had the gun strapped in a holster on my side. I had the coat over it and it was buttoned.

As I walked into the entrance, and tried to enter the concert hall, the security guard approached me. He asked me to open my coat. I started backing up. As I started backing up, he signaled somebody and as I backed up, the San Diego police officers were there. They grabbed me by my arm and opened my coat, discovering the gun. Within seconds, they knew exactly who I was and why I was there. I was so deeply emotionally involved with Robert; I couldn't let go of him. My involvement with him got the best of me, which was the main reason I wanted to kill him; this way no one else could have him. And then I would commit suicide. I was charged with ADW (assault with a deadly weapon) on a person, ex-felon with possession of a firearm, having a gun in a vehicle without a license, and carrying a loaded gun. A jury convicted me on count one, assault with a deadly weapon, and count two, ex-felon with possession of a firearm with two prior felonies. I was given six years in prison.

Folsom Prison

From a distance, it looks like a medieval fortress, surrounded by a four foot wide, ten to twelve foot high Chinese-built wall. As the bus drew up to the back entrance, an iron gate of which I will never forget, I new I had reached the last stop before going to hell. There were several other prisoners on the bus with me and the expressions on their faces were just as frustrated as mine. The gate opened and the bus pulled inside and stopped. A guard came to check the bus occupants and waved it on toward a block stone building.

As we disembarked, I could feel the piercing eyes of other inmates on the other side of the chain link fence. Inmates clad in blue jeans and civilian shirts, others stripped to their waist with ripping biceps from lifting weights, stopped their activities to scrutinize the fresh meat debarking from the bus. There were a lot of eyes on me. I was the youngest of the bunch and feminine looking and I could imagine what was going through their devious minds.

We were taken, in a single file, to a room called Receiving and Release. We stripped and were checked for contraband, given a new set of clothes and the prison's rules and regulations. Then we were assigned housing. I was assigned to Building 2. I had to pass through Building 1 and Dining to get to Building 2.

After reaching Building 2, I was taken to the guard's office where I was told what cell I would be in. Later that day, I found out I had a cellmate. He was Black, a little older than I, somewhat attractive, withdrawn and cautious. We introduced ourselves. His name was James and we talked some about why each of us were incarcerated, and how much time we were facing. Because of my feminine looks and behavior, the inevitable question was "are you gay?" I said yes. The first night, nothing happened. The next day, I went to breakfast, lunch and dinner with him and some of his friends.

That first day, I noticed there was catwalk in front of my cell that ran the full length of the building. There were two tiers of double-bunk cells and the cells bars faced the catwalk. As the guard would walk down the enclosed catwalk with his rifle, he could observe each inmate and every 15 to 20 minutes as he made his pass by each cell.

My second night, James and I had our first sexual encounter and many more were to follow. That first time with James was unforgettable. He was gentle, sweet and loveable, his hands moving slowly over my naked body, his lips softly touching mine and the touch of his tongue as it moved in circles around my nipples. Then I felt him as he entered me, slowly at first, then the motion of his body against mine increased second by second until there was an explosion inside me and his body went limp. As slowly as he entered, he slipped out of me. We both lay there for a few seconds, enjoying the pleasure that flowed through our bodies. We quickly disengaged ourselves because it was time for the guard to make his pass. When the guard reached our cell, James and I were back into out respective bunks, pretending to be asleep.

Before I arrived at Folsom State Prison, I had twice been to Vacaville Medical Facility, and once at Soledad Central for an extended period of time. It was there I learned how to survive in a jungle full of snakes, throat cutters, rats, and sadist perverts. For me, being the only gay on the mainline was dangerous in more ways than one.

There were whites and Mexicans who would have risked their lives (and mine), to have an affair with me. Among the black inmates there was extreme jealousy. These men would do anything to be the main man in my life, and since I chose my cell mate, the one who be that special person, he too would be subjected to pressure as his life was also in great danger.

Being the source of all this madness, I had to walk a thin line and adhere to the jail house Golden Rule: "You see nothing, you hear nothing and you know nothing." If You stick to this rule you survive!

My stay at Folsom was not without incidents. One evening, as James and I were having dinner in the Dining Room, a fight broke out between black and white inmates. Guards stationed at each corner of the Dining Room drew their rifles and began to fire indiscriminately. Bullets were flying all over the place. James and I ducked underneath our table along with other inmates scrambling for cover. Within seconds the Dining Room was crawling with members of the Goon Squad in riot gear. Once the disturbance was under control, we were led back to our respective buildings and placed on lock-down for the rest of the day.

The next day, things were back to normal. I was assigned to a job that was located up the hill from the main buildings. Each morning,

Monday through Friday, I would down to the bottom tier, through the hallway past the Dining Room, through Building 1, into the main yard. I would pass through a chain link fence, pass the weights area, through a locked gate and walk up approximately 100 concrete steps until I reached the top of the hill. I remember the first time I walked to the top of the hill, I turned around and looked back down toward the yard and realized how far I walked. I worked as a clerk in Shipping and Receiving. I did documentation, inventory and inspection. In Shipping and Receiving, inmates made cell lockers for Folsom and other institutions in the Department of Corrections. They also made license plates for the State of California.

One day, at the end of my shift, a guy in the next department called over to me. I went to see what he wanted. I didn't realize until later that he and I were the only ones left except a supervisor who was somewhere else, perhaps securing the area or using the bathroom. While I was talking with him, he sucker punched me in the face, unprovoked. I felt a sharp pain in my jaw. I heard foot stops approaching. The guy disappeared. The supervisor came toward me. I was still stunned by the blow to my face. "Are you ready to go," the supervisor asked me. "Yes," I said. When I got back to my cell, my jaw began to really ache and I decided to go to the hospital.

The doctor examined me and told me I had a broken jaw. I was immediately taken to surgery and the doctor wired my jaw up and placed me into the Hospital Ward. About an hour later, an investigating officer came to question me as to how my jaw got broken. I told the officer, I was getting of my bed to use the toilet when I slipped and fell from the top bunk and struck my head against the railing of the bed. It was a lie—the officer knew was lying—but this is the way things are done in a confined world of convicts. No matter what happened among inmates, you do not rat on one another to the prison's officials.

The head of the BGF (Black Guerilla Family) came and talked with me. I told him exactly what happened. The guy who attacked me was black and prior to the attack, I had no contact with him. I told the BGF member that I think that the guy wanted to sexually assault me by knocking me unconscious. The BGF member told me not to

- 76 -

worry, that they would take care of the situation. I remained on the main line for several months after the attack. I heard rumors as to what happened to the guy who attacked me but I never was able to confirm the rumors. When you are not a rat and you respect other inmates, no matter whether you are straight or gay, you have nothing to fear.

During my work at shipping and receiving I entered a contest. Each person entering the contest was to design a method of constructing a clothes locker where there would not be a metal slip inside the door that could be removed and used as a weapon. I submitted a design that would click with a key, without the metal, that would unlock the lock. I won first prize; they accepted my design and they're still using it today. The only thing they gave me was a certificate.

There was a guy in Folsom named Sheep Thompson. He was vicious, he was dangerous and everyone considered him an animal. Even the police guards were afraid of Sheep Thompson. One day while Sheep Thompson was out on the yard I was there as well. He liked to lift weights and had several friends with whom he lifted weights. This particular day was, you might say, unusual in that a plot had already been set in motion. The plot consisted of two of his weight lifting buddies. He was lifting the weights with one on one side, one on the other. When he went to hand the weight to the guys, they let the weight drop on his chest. Then a third guy came up and stabbed him to death. The guards turned their backs and looked the other way.

Another day while I was working in shipping and receiving, an inmate came in and asked me to help him do something in his department. I went with him to help him. While I was assisting him, he turned around and hit me in the jaw. I was stunned! I didn't go unconscious. Someone came into the room and the guy split. Later on I would find out that he was going to try to rape me by knocking me out. He did not succeed. So that evening when I got off work, I didn't tell anyone. I went back to my cell and realized my jaw was hurt. I had to go to the hospital. The doctor later informed me that I had a broken jaw. Then the guards came. They wanted to know how my jaw got broken. I could not tell them the truth because that would have been snitching. I told them I fell off my bunk and hit my jaw on the commode. Of course they didn't believe it and neither did I. But I stuck to my story and since I didn't name anyone or tell the truth, they had to accept what I told them. They knew that I had had a confrontation with someone and they figured there might be some more repercussions due to the fact I was gay and had made a lot of friends while I was there. They thought it was best that they ship me out. After being there for two years they shipped me to CMC East (California Men's Colony) in 1980.

The California Men's Colony is a country club compared to the other prisons. It is divided into quads: A quad, B quad, C quad and D quad. When I arrived at CMCE (California Men's Colony East) I was housed in A Quad. As I later on found out, A Quad was for the most privileged inmates; they had more freedom than the other quads. B Quad was perhaps one step below A Quad. It mainly consisted of low-riders (young bad boys) and dope addicts. C Quad consisted of mainly PC cases (protected custody individuals who had snitched on other inmates in other prisons were housed in this quad for their protection.) D Quad consisted of inmates who had mental problems or psychological behavior that had to be controlled by some psychotherapy or drugs. My first job at CMC East was working in the lieutenant's office and my duties were to type and file incident reports and assist the Program Lieutenant, a job similar to the one I had when I was incarcerated in Vacaville. While I was there, I met a young man named Eugene Robinson. We became lovers. He was much younger than I and was a little bit immature for his age, too. Our relationship had its ups and downs, but all in all, we managed to stay together; perhaps due to my strong will and determination we made it work.

After being transferred from Folsom, and during my time at CMCE, I met Travis Eugene (Damien) Robinson who became an indelible part of my life at CMCE. It was after I was involved in the incident that took place in the warehouse when another inmate attacked me for sex. It was late in the evening. I was assigned to my dorm and room and was taking a shower, not realizing that someone was watching me. After I came out of the shower, a young man approached me. We began to talk. He asked me if I would go to dinner with him that night. Being new at the facility and not knowing anyone else there, I told him yes.

He was dark ebony, smooth skinned, he had large dark eyes with flaming iris's, lips like black pearls and a body like Michelangelo's David. He was the essence of all I had dreamed of in a man. He was younger than I and he seemed to depend on me as his protector from the evil environment that surrounded us. There were guys there who were bullies that would have taken advantage of him if it weren't for me. Our relationship lasted for about two years when I discovered that I had gotten a reversal on my latest conviction and I was remanded back to court to either be retried or released. During these two years we were always together; going to dinners, movies and playing sports in the yard; or, just sitting around drinking coffee. I remember one time he approached me and told me some guy wanted to do some harm to him. He said he had been gambling and he had lost some money. The guy wanted to be paid and he didn't have any money. Since you cannot have real money in prison, cigarettes become legal tender. I asked him the guy's name. I told him not to worry, that I would take care of the problem. I could see in his eyes that he was very afraid that they were going to hurt him because in prison, cigarettes are extremely valuable and if you owe someone a debt and do not pay, they will kill you. I have known of times where individuals were killed over a pack of cigarettes. I talked to the guy to whom the debt was owed and found out that Travis (nicknamed Damien) owed two cartons of cigarettes; so I paid him off. After that little incident I talked to Damien and he stopped gambling. Things went smoothly until I was sent back to San Diego on the reversal of my charges.

While I was at CMC East, the appellate court was hearing the appeal on my conviction. When they reached a decision, I had been at CMC East for almost two years. I received the decision of the court in the office of the program lieutenant. The lieutenant told me that the court had reversed my conviction and that I would be leaving within two weeks, going back to San Diego. During this conversation with the lieutenant I was told that no matter what happened, and because of my record and my anger against the system, he would give me six weeks and I'd be back in prison again. I looked the lieutenant in the eye and told him, "Don't hold your breath because I won't be back." And I left the office. It was almost two weeks before I was released and returned to San Diego. Just before I left CMC East, Eugene and I talked about the future. He was in for murder and there seemed to be no chance that he would be getting out soon. We, however, agreed to keep up our relationship and I would correspond with him when I was released.

When I returned to San Diego I was confined at the San Diego County Jail until they called a hearing in my case. There was still the remaining charge of ex-felon with possession of a firearm that had to be settled by the court. The District Attorney informed me that they were going to dismiss the original charge of assault with a deadly weapon and an ex-felony possession of a firearm providing that I plead guilty to possession of a firearm by a felon (the second gun). They would give me time served on that count and I would be released. I accepted the deal and was released three days later.

David Ray Brown

David, CNA,
Mercy Rehab Hospital

David, Liz & Vince Ninteman

Borrego Springs

Borrego Springs

Aphram, Westin Hotel, 2006

David & Aphram

Coast Hotel, Still located at 7th & Island
in Downtown San Diego

This is the window where the Sailor jumped
through during the shooting.

Maria Galleta

Jennifer
Waitress, Marie's Cafe

Pat Washington & Jess San Roque

The Ninteman's Family
Vince, Margie&Daughter Cherie & David

David, Marie & Friends

David's 65 Birthday Party

Demetric Cook, David, Dimetric's Wife & Boys

Eddie Cong

Aphram Woldeyes
My Adopted Son

David R. Brown
Being Alive

David
Adam Street Fair, 2006

Demetric Green

Robert Ray Davis

Francis & Althea

Clyde Breland
My Beloved Brother

Jimmy Rutherford

Sabrina Rubalcava

Erik & Girlfriend Stephanie

Stephanie & David

Aunt Bette

David R. Brown

La Princess Charmagne

CHAPTER SIX

Years later, Sam and I would resume our relationship as brothers. We were both on the streets and he was still wheeling and dealing. During the 1980's, I assisted him with a couple of legal proceedings that he had going on with the District Attorney's office. Due to my illness, I dropped out of law classes at San Diego City College and started a paralegal business. The cases that I worked on with my brother involved narcotics. I would go to his apartment next door to mine and talk to him, advising him on his legal problems. During these sessions, I noticed that he had a lot of expensive jewelry, antiques and paintings. Knowing that he was not employed, I guessed that he was involved in some form of illegal activities, but I didn't have any definitive, inside knowledge of it.

I remember one particular incident when Sam owned an antique shop on First and University. He lived above the shop. One night the police broke in through the security gate and searched his apartment. They found several ounces of cocaine. He called me from jail and I got him out on bail. The case dragged on for years. I don't remember the outcome of it, but I do know that he did not do any time. As of this date, he lives in a home in the Clairemont area of San Diego that he bought several years ago. I have been to his home in Clairemont several times. His house is full of antiques, novelties and a huge iron safe. I remember one time he opened his safe and there was a lot of cash inside of it. His house has been broken into by the police a couple of times recently, yet he still has been able to evade incarceration. It makes me believe that he has some connection with organized crime or has some "juice" with law enforcement. After the debacle of the selling of my mother's home, I decided to break ties with Sam. For the past 23 years, I have been free from any contact with the police. I have not broken the law and have not been to jail since 1983. My dealings with my brother, Sam, in assisting him with his legal problems, ceased when I decided it was time for me to stay clear of him, and to insure that I would not have any problems with police or involved with the judicial system again.

I was raised in a very dysfunctional family. There were always problems among my siblings. All but two of us had different fathers. I never knew my father and every time I asked about him my mother would become very agitated and tell me to mind my own business. I once asked my Aunt Bette. She tried to explain to me about my father but I got the impression that she did not really know herself. For years I suffered from the agony of not knowing whom my father was and if he were still alive.

My relationship with my oldest brother, Sam, was intolerable. We remained at a distance from one another and still do, even to this day. He always acted as though he were superior to those around him; and superior to me. I never forgave him for his aloofness toward me. He had a way of controlling others around him. To my knowledge he has never had a job. There was some indication that he had attended law school at one time, but there is no proof that he ever did. He is a very manipulative person, self-centered and devoid of any compassion for others.

My second brother, Bobby, suffered a great deal from the rejection and lack of love of growing up in a dysfunctional family. Being the third brother, he had no one to look up to and no positive role model to guide him. Having two older brothers, who were not only gay but who also didn't communicate with each other, played an important role in his overall behavior. He is also self-centered, argumentative and very hard to get along with. He always boasts about how much money he makes and how much money he wins at the racetrack. For most of his life he worked at Del Mar Race Track. He retired from there and won a lot of money playing the horses. He had several girlfriends but none of those relationships lasted very long. He once was involved intimately with my friend, Thomas Rubalcava, better known as Sabrina. He and Sabrina stayed with me for a while. Other than his affair with Sabrina, I never knew him to be involved in a homosexual relationship again. A couple of years ago he suffered at least two heart attacks and as a result is in poor health. I see him about twice a week at Marie's Cafe in North Park. We have never had a good relationship as brothers and he has never been a guest in my home. He never married.

Clyde, my third brother, was my favorite. I remember when he was born and my mother brought him home. It became my responsibility to make his formula and to change his diapers, and look after him. Clyde was a very good kid. I really don't know who his father was but there were rumors that his father was one of the Wallace boys that lived up the street from us. He did have the resemblance and the skin color of the Wallace siblings. When I went back to California in 1957, Clyde, Bobby, Sam and two of my youngest brothers were living in Logan Heights. Later on, Clyde joined the Navy and was sent to Vietnam. He spent close to two years in the war. When he was discharged he was suffering from severe shell shock. By this time my mother had married for the first time. Her husband, Bill Green, was a stucco worker. He bought my mother a home in Emerald Hills. Clyde stayed with my mother after his discharge from the Navy. Clyde was a heavy drinker and smoker. At the time of his discharge he was receiving approximately $900 a month as a Vietnam War Veteran. His drinking and smoking got so bad that by the end of the month, most of the time, he didn't have a dime left after paying my mother rent and buying food. Clyde and I had an unusual relationship as brothers. Before his untimely death, we became even closer as brothers. Therefore, his passing was indeed stressful and heartbreaking to me. To this day, memories of him still haunt me and many nights I find myself alone thinking of him, and I am sure that where ever he is, he is thinking about me. I truly pray that God forgave us both for our sins.

I was headed north on 54th Street towards El Cajon Boulevard to the Lucky Lady Casino when I noticed a little blonde girl wandering aimlessly down the street in front of me. My first thought was to keep walking and mind my own business. Every time I have tried to help someone for whatever reason it may have been, I have ended up in trouble. Seeing this young girl, knowing that she was alone and possibly lost, I could not ignore her. I walked up to her and asked her name, she was very shy and did not respond right away, only when I asked her where she lived she responded by pointing up the street, south from where she was walking. "Where are your mom and dad?" I asked her. She made a quizzical face. It appeared she was not going to talk so I decided to take a different approach. I took her by the hand and told her to take me to her house. She started walking south and finally stopped at a house that had steps leading to a front door that was open and I could see flashes of lights from what appeared to be a television.

I took her up the steps to the open door, there was a screen door closed but not latched. I knocked on the screen door a couple of times. When there was no answer I asked, "Is anyone home?" No answer. I opened the door and went in. I went into the living room, the television was on and a young boy about the age of fourteen or fifteen was lying on a sofa asleep. I woke him up and he appeared startled at first but seemed to relax when I explained why I was there. He said that the young girl was his sister and his mother had left her in his care while she went downtown to the County Jail to see about her boyfriend who had been arrested by the police. I told him that his sister was down the street walking in the dark alone and that it was unsafe for her to be alone in the streets. He told me that he had fallen asleep and thought she was in her bedroom. He had no idea that she had left the house. He promised me that he would watch her closely until his mother came back home.

I left the two of them and continued on my journey to the Casino. I kept thinking to myself did I do the right thing? What would have happened if someone had called the police? Would I have been accused of trying to kidnap this girl? Would the police convince the young boy to make false statements against me? These thoughts and others like them raced through my head as I walked in the dark. Over the years I often wondered what happened to that young lady?

Does she remember that night and does she remember me? Maybe I should have reported this incident to the police but my decision not to was due to my fear of the police. This fear is deep rooted in my distrust of the police due to my previous encounters with law enforcement. I'm certain it had much to do with my illegal arrests in 1964 and 1968 for the sale of marijuana, and for an infamous crimes of kidnapping and assault with a deadly weapon, in 1967. Reflecting back to the events that occurred that night, and my decision not to report it to the police, I believe that I did the right thing.

Later when I was paroled in 1974, I did not resume my friendship with

Miss Frances immediately and as a result, our friendship soon vanished. It was only in 1981, after being released from prison the third time that I ran into Miss Frances again. At that time she and Miss Althea were running around together. Miss Althea lived around the corner from my mother's house. I didn't know her well but had seen her off and on several times. I did know that my mother and Althea's mother knew each other and that Althea also knew my youngest brother, Clyde. I was told at one time that she and Clyde were having an affair or had had an affair.

In the early 1980s, I was involved with someone else and attending college at night, working two jobs during the day. I did not have much time to run around with Miss Frances. So we, for the most part, went our separate ways. It was only in the early 90's that I ran into Frances and Althea again. At this time, they were sharing an apartment in the Logan Heights area. Someone had told me that Miss Frances and Althea both had contracted AIDS. There were times during this period that I would stop by their apartment and visit with them. Also during this time, I was carrying the HIV virus myself, but it had not developed into AIDS. A few years later, I was informed by my brother, Clyde, that Miss Frances had passed away from complications of AIDS and a week later he told me that Miss Althea had also passed away of AIDS.

Gambling became my favorite pastime in the ensuing years. I loved the thrill of winning but there were also many times that I lost. I remember the first hand that I ever played. I was dealt four queens at a card room on Fifth and Island, called The Rose Card Room. I did not realize the potential of the hand I was holding until my friend, who was sitting beside me, nudged me and told me that I had one of the best hands possible. I won the pot. That was the beginning of my gambling. Later on I began to patronize the Lucky Lady Card Room on El Cajon Boulevard. I was a constant customer at the Card Room. Like most gamblers, some nights I would win a lot of money; other nights I would lose some. No one in the card room knew my sexual identity. Everyone thought I was a lady. I began to get acquainted with people that eventually would turn into lifelong friends.

The Lucky Lady Card Room was unique. It was the gathering place for some of the best gamblers in San Diego, members of organized crime and other scam artists could also be found there. It was here at this card room that I first met Tommy Tampezee, his brother, Ace, and John Zarelle. Later on I would work for John Zarelle as a manager for his record shop in downtown San Diego. I worked for John as Princess Charmagne; they didn't know the real truth. John would eventually sell his record shop because of some legal problems he was having with the Feds. He eventually moved from San Diego to Seattle, Washington. I continued to play cards at the Lucky Lady and began to make a reputation as one of the best poker players in San Diego.

One night while at the Lucky Lady, two detectives came in and arrested me on an outstanding warrant. I had failed to appear in court on a charge of prostitution. When I was arrested that night, the detective told the owner that I was a female impersonator. That's how everyone found out that I was not a woman but a man. Everybody was shocked and surprised. They just couldn't believe the reality of my being a man. Even to this day there are people who still tell others about those times when I used to come into the card room and no one knew I was a man. I still play cards at the Lucky Lady today and there are many people there who remember me from years past. I will always remember Tommy and Ace Tampezee. Tommy was rumored to be a member of the San Diego Organized Crime family. It was common knowledge that heart problems within the Tampezee family were hereditary. A few years ago Ace passed away from a heart attack and a few weeks later Tommy passed away, also from a heart attack.

The Lucky Lady was always my favorite card room. Even after they found out I was a man dressed in women's clothes, I was always respected and welcomed there. Some of the people I used to know at the Lucky Lady in addition to Ace and Tommy have also passed away. One of the most remarkable that I knew was a dealer named Julie. She was Filipino and always had a smile on her face. She recently passed away from a brain aneurysm. She was only in her early 40's. I did not find out about her death until a few weeks after she had died. It was a terrible shock to me because we were very close friends. I can still remember going into the Lucky Lady when she would greet me with a smile and talk to me and tell me how wonderful I was. Sometimes she would accompany me to the Indian Casinos and we would spend all night gambling and having a ball!

The Palomar Club is another card room where Julie and I would go. There were many people there with whom we became friends. One was Tippy. He was a gentleman in his early 80's who would tell me many stories about people he had met in the past, and we would also discuss the O'Connor family.

I told him about working for Maureen O'Connor when she was running for mayor of San Diego. He would tell me that he knew her father, Jerome O'Connor, when he was a boxer in the 40's. I, too, remember Jerome O'Connor. I remember sitting with him sometimes at the courthouse; other times at Horton Plaza where we would discuss law issues while I was attending law school. It was through him that I met his daughter, Maureen. Jerome was perhaps one of the greatest legal minds I have ever known. He was smart, an intellectual who knew a great deal about law, perhaps because of his ability to sit for long periods of time in a courtroom several times a week.

There were many other well-known people I met at the Palomar Club - lawyers, doctors and assistants to councilmen. One of my most unforgettable friends at the Palomar Club was David Woods. He was a coffee boy (another name for gopher). Before he became a gopher, David had worked for a legal firm in downtown San Diego. He had fallen from grace due to his heavy drinking. I found it hard to believe that a person with his knowledge and his high standing in the community, would allow himself to sink so low to become a coffee boy. His income from working at the Palomar Club was perhaps a third of the money he was making when he was working as a paralegal. We became very close friends although there were many times we had heated debates on issues of law. Many times I would preach to him about his heavy drinking and question him as to why he put up with so much degradation from the players and from his boss. They treated him like a dog, making him run here and there and fix this and that. David and I still remain friends, but he no longer works for the Palomar Club. I don't know if he ever quit drinking.

Barney had a very unusual personality. He became one of my friends at the Palomar Club. He was an ex-serviceman who had an answer for every question you asked him. The most notable trait of his personality was his foul mouth. He would cuss consistently and he never showed any respect for anyone he met. He had a girlfriend who was Iranian and she seemed to put up with his profane attitude. I once asked her what she saw in him and she told me that he was just a homeless scared little boy and that the only way he felt important was to make everyone else seem smaller than he. After I got to know him personally, I realized what she was saying was true. Now that he has passed away, many people miss his presence, and perhaps his colorful language.

Lincoln was another very good friend of mine. He was from Jamaica. He was considered a high roller; a youngster of about 26 years old, driving a brand new leased car every other night. These were Cadillacs, BMWs, Lincolns or Mercedes.

He was always with young ladies dressed in the best clothes, looking like high-priced prostitutes. It was quite obvious what business he was in. He could not possibly have a job because he was always in the card room gambling, talking and drinking. I did some legal work for him once. He paid me very well for filing some legal papers to stay in this country and as of this day he is still in America. I don't know if he has become an American citizen yet. I saw him recently and bought him a drink at the Palomar. We discussed a few things and I came to the conclusion that he had changed most of his ways. His gambling became a financial crisis for him. It seems he lost his money and was no longer able to afford the life of a high-roller.

The last time I was at the Palomar, I got into an argument with one of the dealers and I threatened him. I told him if he would go outside with me I would do some harm to him. He jumped up on the table and called the floor man. He told the floor man that I was going home to get my gun and come back and shoot him. This may have been what I was thinking, but it is not what I said. Later on, after I had cashed my chips out and walked outside the card room, a security guard told me I was "86'd" from the club and I have not been back since.

CHAPTER SEVEN

From 1976 to 1978 I worked for the Ninteman Construction Company. The first day on the jobsite was quite memorable. I was sent there from the Union Hall, Local 89. I was supposed to be there for two days only. The first day, I was instructed to dig a trench for plumbing at a construction site where a new bank was to be built. At the end of the shift and after working for eight hours, I was told by the labor foreman to report to the construction yard the next day. He explained to me that the owner, L.J. Ninteman, had been watching me for a couple of hours and he liked the way I worked. He wanted to see me personally at the yard office at 8:00 a.m. the next day.

I reported to the office and I met Mr. Ninteman for the first time. He was an older gentleman about six feet tall with a slight German accent. He wore prescription eyeglasses that gave him a very distinguished look. He said, "I noticed you working and the way you were digging that trench. I have never seen anyone so consistent in digging a hole." He asked, "How much education do you have?" I told him I had one year of college. Then he explained to me what he wanted me to do. He gave me a yellow legal size tablet and lead pencil. He said I want you to inventory everything in the shop from the largest machine to the smallest of nails. I took the tablet and pencil and I finished the project within three hours. After I finished I gave him the inventory list. He looked at it for several seconds and then he said, "I have never seen anyone with such penmanship." Where did you learn to print so well? I told him I did not know; I guessed it was a natural gift.

He then said, "I'm going to put you in charge of the yard. You will be my yardman and you will work along with an Italian artist working on a special project for the City of San Diego. The next day, I learned what the special project was. It was restoring art pieces that had been cut from the old aerospace museum in Balboa Park. My job would be to assist the artist in restoring these pieces with plaster of Paris and afterwards the restored pieces would be cast into fiberglass. There were approximately two hundred pieces that had to be restored and molds were needed for recasting. After two weeks and approximately 25 pieces that were completely restored, VJ came to me and told me that he was taking the artist off the project and I would be taking over as the main artist (The reason for this move was because I later told him about my artistic ability as a kid, and my quick learning in restoring the pieces). I'm sure that the fact that the artist was costing him $17 per hour and I was being paid much less, more like $9.00 an hour, was the real reason. I can hardly blame him. It was an economical move.

One day while working at the shop restoring these pieces there was a commotion up front. As I turned around and looked toward the front entrance of the shop I saw television cameras and several people coming toward me. Mr. Ninteman was talking to one of the reporters trying to find out what was going on. I heard him tell one of the reporters that the art piece I was working on was supposed to be a secret project. No one was to know about it. I heard the reporter say to Mr. Ninteman that they were not concerned about the art pieces. They wanted to interview me. Someone had informed them of my affiliation with the SLA and at that same time they had Patty Hearst in jail in San Diego at the MCC, (Metropolitan Correction Center) downtown.

The reporter's interview:
EX-CONVICT FINDS NEW LIFE IN SAN DIEGO

> *As if carefully holding a baby, a laborer examined several large plaster of Paris statues and columns.*

> *He continued to study the plaster pieces, which he had made earlier, as a visitor an approached him inside a warehouse in the Morena area. The plaster pieces are exact replicas of those destroyed by the Electric Building fire and will adorn the exterior of the new Aero-Space Museum.*

> *A few minutes later, the man paused and said, "I'm doing something that probably will last a long time, and many people after me will enjoy seeing them for generations to come.*

> *"It makes me feel good I had a hand in having done it, because I know it's important."*

> *The man is David Brown, 34, a former convict and prison-*

-mate of Donald DeFreeze. Together in Vacaville Prison, they organized a group of inmates that later spawned the Symbionese Liberation Army.

Brown came back to San Diego after spending ten long and violent years in state prisons. His mother and six brothers had come from Mississippi when he was a young boy, and he later attended San Diego High.

Released from Soledad prison in late 1974, Brown arrived here ready to start life again. He hit the pavement, determined to find employment and, sometime later, landed a job in a downtown restaurant.

Now a laborer, Brown recalled the beginning of what was to be known as the SLA. We were members of the Black Cultural Association in 1972, and we organized the SLA because we wanted a more political-minded group," Brown said. "The BCA was under the jurisdiction of the prison officials and you couldn't say what you wanted."

"So DeFreeze, a brother named Death Row Jeff and myself formed the SLA secretly.

Later, he said, outside visitors came into Vacaville to teach and attend BCA-sponsored education classes. Here contact began with outside individuals who were sympathetic toward our political philosophy and later some of the visitors were identified as members of radical groups, which eventually led to the disbanding of the BCA and the SLA. Brown estimated that there were at least 100 SLA members in prison at that time. The leaders of the SLA were identified by prison officials, were locked up and transferred to different prisons within the Department of Corrections. Donald Defreeze and I were transferred to Soledad Central.

Shortly after arriving at Soledad, DeFreeze escaped, linked up with his numerous contacts made while at Vacaville and then burst into the public's eye with the kidnapping of heiress Patricia Hearst.

'We never did agree on the methods of how to achieve a successful political struggle in this country," Brown said of himself and DeFreeze. "He had his own methods, and I had my own methods."

"He was too impatient, and that's one thing that contributed to his being killed off. He should have waited and planned things out much better than he did."

Brown, an accomplished artist and writer, says he would like to write a book on "the inception of the SLA."

"From the time in the penitentiary, I've learned a great deal. I improved myself and got more education than if I had stayed on the streets.

"I view that time as past history, but I can feel better about myself, and I know I can think better."

Approximately two weeks after the interview, I was informed by an attorney, Mr. Robert McMillan, who was a friend of mine that F. Lee Bailey the attorney for Patty Hearst had contacted him and wanted to interview me.

I said to my friend the attorney, if I was going to be interviewed by Mr. Bailey, that I wanted him present and it had to be a private/secret meeting. I wanted to remain anonymous.

Three days later, McMillan called me and said that he had set up an appointment and that Mr. Bailey and William Randolph Hearst, Patty Hearst's father, would meet us at the San Diego International Airport in the VIP lounge cafeteria. There were five of us - my attorney, Mr. Bailey, Mr. Hearst, Ms. Jiminez and myself. Ms. Jiminez was Patty Hearst's private guard (Patty had a private guard even while imprisoned. She later married her second guard. They allowed her to have a male guard in the women's prison. Actually, it was more like a country club. After all, who was going to argue with William Randolph Hearst, one of the richest men in the country? He wanted his daughter protected.)

I was amazed by my first impression of F. Lee Bailey and William Randolph Hearst. Mr. Bailey was shorter than I thought he would be and did not actually measure up to what I had expected him to be as a famed defense attorney. Mr. Hearst was tall and not as distinguished looking as I thought he would be. I was not intimidated by either man, and the interview proceeded. They asked me several questions about brainwashing and asked whether we as an organization taught brainwashing techniques. I told them that all Symbionese Liberation Party members were required to study brainwashing principles and the philosophy of Brigit Debray, the red book of Moa Tsung and Chico Riviera. They asked me if I believed Patty Hearst was brainwashed. I told them it was possible because Donald DeFreeze was well versed in brainwashing techniques. They asked me if I would testify on behalf of Patty Hearst. I told them I would have to discuss it further with my attorney. After some questioning about the ins and outs of brainwashing, the interview was over.

I talked briefly with Jiminez before I left and she brought up the subject of my writing a book about my life. She said she would assist me, but I never heard from her again. Somehow the news media found out about the meeting but only after it was over. There was a brief write-up the next day in the San Diego Union Tribune about "an unidentified person with his attorney who met with F. Lee Bailey and William Randolph Hearst at Lindbergh Field."

CHAPTER EIGHT

The years I spent with Robert, including our many trials and tribulations, will forever linger in my soul. Our sexual encounters were unique and very enjoyable. I have had affairs, relationships and sexual encounters with many men, past and present, but none to the depths of emotion and passion I shared with Robert. Robert was everything to me; my heart, soul and body. I often told myself, much like the song, "If loving you is wrong, I don't wanna be right". It's the main reason I wanted to kill him when he left me. Many nights as I lay awake after he was gone I cried and wondered with whom he was sleeping. I am truly grateful to this day that I did not kill him, or myself, as I had planned, because today we are still friends and shall always remain.

I was found guilty of assault with a deadly weapon (ADW) and an ex-felon in possession of a firearm, and sentenced to six years in prison. The case was then appealed. The Fourth Appellate District Division Number 1, State of California, stated that the police statement said that I pulled the trigger. Only a click was heard. There was no sign of bullets and no spent cartridge was recovered. The detective also stated that there were shots fired from the gun, but again, no spent cartridge was ever recovered. I had previously stated that what appeared to be a gun in my possession was not a real gun. It was toy gun. The appellate court decided to reverse the conviction due to the fact that what I stated was true, because the detectives found no spent cartridge. The following day when I appeared at the concert with a new gun, which was a real gun in my possession, I violated the law because I was an ex-felon with a gun. Finally, I was released from prison on the reversal and was allowed to plead guilty to possession of the second weapon with the charges of assault dismissed. This took place in 1981. I was in prison for approximately two years before my appeal was heard.

Robert was probably the first person I really loved; and he loved me, too. We had a good relationship for the first couple of years. When I got out of prison in 1981, after trying to kill him, Robert was still living in San Diego. He was staying with one of his sisters on El Cajon Blvd when I ran into him again. We talked about old times and I apologized for what I tried to do to him. We continued to see each other. However, we never resumed our relationship but remained close friends. Robert was in and out of jail for petty stuff but mainly for drugs for the next several months. Each time he was sent to jail he would call. One day he called me and asked me if he could spend a couple nights at my place. He told me that he had just gotten out of jail and had no place to stay. I let him come over to my apartment where he spent two nights.

I remember a friend of mine saying to me afterwards that I must be crazy to let Robert stay with me after I had tried to kill him. I told my friend that I wasn't afraid of Robert; he should be more afraid of me and that he was crazy for coming to stay with me! A couple of years later Robert returned to prison for a petty crime he had committed. Since he was a "twice convicted felon" and already had several misdemeanors, he was eventually convicted under the three-strike-law and sentenced to life in prison.

Recently I received a letter from him. He wanted me to help support the initiative of reversing the three strike law, which did not pass during the election. It was defeated mainly through the efforts of the Governor of the State of California. I also sent him money to buy a television, which I doubt he bought because after all the years he had been in prison, he could have already acquired one. I am quite sure that when he is released, if ever, he will come back to San Diego and I will see him again. I truly believe that he is the first man that I ever loved, and still love, and will continue to love. We shared so much together in the two and a half years we were together.

I first met William Thompson in the late 1970's when Robert and I were living on Van Dyke Street in City Heights. Bill was an older gentleman, well dressed and appeared to be a businessman. We would hang out together at different places; coffee shops, peep arcades, etcetera. I later learned that Bill owned a real estate company on Market Street and he was a good friend of my Aunt Bette's. During a time when Robert and I had separated because of some problems we were having in our relationship, I found out that he was staying with Mr. Thompson. I went to Bill's house and we had words. I told him to leave Robert alone. Robert came back home several days later.

Thompson later purchased the Voice and View Point Newspaper, a black publication that was on the verge of bankruptcy. We were not close friends but our paths crossed occasionally, especially at the peep show on 5th and G Street. Bill lived in Emerald Hills on Roswell Street a few blocks from my mother's home and right across the street from Miss Peaches' home. After he purchased the Voice and View Point, he remodeled his home on top of the hill on Roswell and it became one of the showcase homes in Emerald Hills. When I heard the news about his death and how he was killed, I was sure I knew right away what had happened. The police report said he was stabbed many, many times in his bedroom and there appeared to be no forcible entry to the home. His car was missing and it was my assumption that he probably picked up one of the young hustlers who hung around the peep show on Fifth Avenue and took him home. While in the bedroom something went wrong. Perhaps an inappropriate pass was made toward the young man or an argument ensued over money that could have sparked the outburst of violence. This led to Mr. Thompson's death. When the murder occurred my first reaction was that Robert had had a hand in it, but later on I was proven to be wrong. Whatever happened, I am sure Bill was not able to defend himself from the vicious attack by his killer.

I called my Aunt Bette and told her of Bill's death. She was devastated. Mr. Thompson had helped Aunt Bette in her real estate transactions and they remained friends. The detectives followed many leads but all of them came to a dead end. I once told the detectives right after Bill's death what I thought had happened and why. Many years have passed and in 2005 they finally apprehended the killer. Since there was no DNA technology available when he was murdered all leads went cold. While going through some cold case files the detectives decided to run blood samples collected at the scene of the murder, through the DNA national database and they got a hit. The suspect was doing time in a California prison. They brought him back to San Diego and charged him with the murder of Mr. William Thompson. As soon as I heard the news, I again called my Aunt Bette and told her that they had found Bill's killer. I told her to watch the 6:00 news on Channel 10! I gave her all the information I had at the time and she was elated saying,

"Thank God, they caught him!" At the time of this writing the case against the suspect is pending.

CHAPTER NINE

In 1982, I had just been released from CMC-East a year before. While I was incarcerated in CMC-East, I was having an affair with Travis Eugene Robinson (Damien). Travis had given me his brother's name and social security number. I took these to the motor vehicle department and had my picture placed on an identification card with his brother's name and Social Security number on it. Travis had been transferred to San Quentin. From there he wrote and told me that I could come and visit him as his brother. I would be able to come inside the prison and stay for two days alone with him. Clyde asked to accompany me on my trip to San Quentin State Prison. We arrived in Monterey, California, a small community by the prison and I rented a motel room for the night. The next day, before I left for the prison to spend a couple of days with Travis, Clyde begged to go with me. I told him he couldn't. He became emotionally distraught because I was leaving him. He asked me to go to bed with him before I left. I hesitated at first but I saw how serious he was and I gave in to his request.

Clyde was not a homosexual; he was actually more of a bi-sexual. He had fleeting relationships with women, but he liked to go with me to the gay bars and enjoyed being around my gay friends. Sometimes he would leave with one of them, go home and I would not see him again for a couple of days. It was years later when I realized Clyde had become emotionally attached to me. I remember several times that I would come to my mother's house where he was living and bring a friend. He would be angry and would go off cussing and calling me names. His behavior was even more violent in nature when my friend was white. On those occasions he would want to jump the guy and would show a lot of jealousy because the guy was with me. No matter what happened in the years until his death, he would always come back to me for help and I was always there for him. His death was a terrible blow to me. He never married and never had any known children.

Carl, my fourth brother was 21 years younger than I and was the quiet one. He was inquisitive, studious and ambitions. Because of the vast age difference, I was not around him much as a child. As he grew up my most unforgettable memory of him was of the innocent little boy holding my mother's hand, crying, when I came to the house the evening my mother informed me of Bill's fiasco in Las Vegas and losing all their money. It was only after he had finished High School and began working for the Navy as a civilian that I came in contact with him again. There were my occasional visits to my mother's home when he was present, but we never had very much to say to each other.

However, while Carl was working for the Navy we began to communicate with each other as brothers. I remember once he came to my birthday party when Robert and I were living together. That evening at the party I will never forget what he said to one of my guests. I was most proud of him when one of my guests tried to put the "make" on him and he told this individual, "I know my brother is gay and I respect him. I am not gay so you must respect me." That's when I intervened and told my guest that he must refrain from his inappropriate behavior or he would have to leave. Between Carl and Clyde, it is almost impossible for me to say which was dearer to my heart. Carl was very handsome and had a lot of sex appeal, yet there was some hidden frustration and bitterness from being a part of such a dysfunctional family. I have always loved and admired Carl. He is the only one of all my brothers who had acquired a decent education and pursued a career that enabled him to better his life. Most of my other siblings could barely read or write and none of them ever attained a high school education. He has girlfriends but never married. I just recently learned he has a daughter. The last I heard he was living near Lemon Grove, California.

Then there's Glen, my fifth brother. He is perhaps the most troublesome of us all. Like Carl, I was not around him much as he grew up. But there was one incident that I remember very well. My mother threw him out of the house when he was 15 years old and he came to stay with me. He was having drug addiction problems which worsened. My mother could no longer handle him, so she kicked him out of the house. About the same time he was kicked out of mom's house, his girlfriend, Regina, was also kicked out of her mother's house. Regina was working for the Navy when Glen met her. She was not into drugs until she met him. He turned her on and she, too, became addicted.

They both ended up staying with me. A few days after they moved in, someone told my mother. She called me on the phone and told me I was a bad influence on my brother and she did not like the idea of him staying with me. When I told her that she had kicked him out of her house and because he is my brother, he has a right to stay with me. She threatened to send the police to my house if Glen continued to stay with me. Two days later the police knocked on my door and asked to speak with me about my brother, Glen. They told me that my mother had told them that I was a homosexual and that she was afraid that my brother would be influenced by me. I told the police that their concern was unwarranted and that Glen was my brother. If he chose to stay with me, it was no business of theirs. I told them the next time they came to my house, please have a warrant and I closed the door in their face. That was the last I heard from them. Glen and Regina lived with me for about eight months.

Over the next few years, I helped Glen financially due to the many offspring he was having all over the place. He not only had two sons by Regina, his girlfriend, he had several other children all over San Diego. He had a daughter by one girl, twin boys by another girl and he had two other sons by another girl. How many more I don't even know. He seemed to always find himself in a situation where I would either have to bail him out or help support some of his kids. His two sons by Regina, Dimetri and Glen, Jr., I practically raised myself. They lived with me off and on. Regina had no job, no income, no place to live so the children had to live with their grandmother. I helped her with them.

The first son, Dimetri, received a football scholarship at the University of Michigan and graduated from there. He met and married a girl there and she will graduate in the spring of 2005. He was taking a Paramedic Course. I agreed to send him money as long as he remains in school. The second son, Glen, Jr. has a drug problem and has been kicked out of his grandmother's house. He works and keeps a job. He doesn't have the education his older brother has. He took some college courses at Grossmont College in La Mesa. Most of the time they lived with their maternal grandmother. They still, however, see their mother, Regina.

In his late 30's and after years of running around fraternizing with young ladies and having babies, Paul Sr. finally got married in 2004 to a young lady named Lisa. They didn't have any children as of this writing and he's still running around chasing other women, using drugs and is unemployed. The marriage to Lisa is a puzzle to me. From the time they got married and up to this day, they have never lived together as husband and wife, although he does see her. They do have some type of relationship, but no one can figure out what it is. Just recently he tried to commit suicide and was committed to a psych unit. He has since been released and is back on the streets still unemployed.

My brother Glen, who was always in trouble with the law, finally was facing the three-strike law. California's three-strike law in plain English says, "A person who has committed two felonies and facing a charge or charges which add up to another felony conviction, could be subject to the three-strike law". If that person is convicted under the three-strike law, he could be sentenced to life in prison. Such a decision to try a person under the law in some cases can be left up to the discretion of the judge. Glen escaped the three-strike law, as I was later told, by promising the court that he had found Christ and that if the court would give him another chance, he would become a productive citizen and refrain from crime.

He was eventually released on probation and is now living in Chula Vista, California, with two other guys. I later learned that the two guys that were staying with him were placed into his care by his girlfriend, Lisa, who later became his wife. One of the guys was Lisa's brother and the other her cousin. They both suffered from depression and took prescribed medications and were on Social Security. Glen's responsibilities were to make sure that they took their medication on time and control most of their money. Glen was also on Social Security and was receiving some type of disability payment for a back ailment that he claimed he suffered from a job related incident.

After being released he became an ordained minister. When I was told about his ordination, I became skeptical because of his past history of deception and conniving ways. I did not believe that he was sincere about being a minister and I had my doubts about his sincerity. I was invited to hear him preach a couple of times at a church in Emerald Hills where my cousin Reverend Manley is pastor. My cousin was in. As I listened to my brother's sermon, I had even more doubts as to his dedication as a minister, yet I wanted to give him the benefit of the doubt. A few months later I received a call from him and he told me that the manager of the motel they were staying in had asked them to move or be faced with eviction. The reason for this, it seemed, was that one of the guys had caused a disturbance at the motel and the manager asked them to move. Glen asked if they could come and stay with me for a couple of weeks until they could find another place to stay. At first I hesitated and told him he needed to give me a few days to give him an answer. After consulting with my Aunt Bette, I called Glen back and offered him my place until he was able to secure his own living quarters. What followed was a nightmare that I will never forget.

After Glen moved in with the two guys he was living with, I being a good natured person, knowing he had a back problem and problems with his knees, decided to let him use the bedroom while the other guys could sleep in the living room with me. At night these guys would make their beds on the floor and for the first few nights things seemed to be going all right. As the days passed, though, I began to notice that my silverware appeared to have been caught in the garbage disposal and some of my glasses and dishes were disappearing, perhaps broken. I began to have problems communicating with them about keeping the house clean and keeping the noise down when they were listening to music. They seemed to have no consideration for the neighbors. Finally I began to have verbal confrontations with my brother about the cleanliness of the bathroom, silverware that had been caught in the disposal and the noise they had been making when I was not at home. There were a few instances when I would come back home in the evening. I would hear loud voices and religious music all the way to the front gate of the apartment complex.

One time I approached him about the situation and he told me that I had no right to tell him what to do. Then he threatened me. I proceeded to tell him that this was my house and not his; that I had a right to tell him what I felt in my own house. He became very angry and pushed me against the wall. Knowing his background and that he had a black belt in Judo, and remembering also one time years earlier when the police tried to arrest him, two policemen ended up in the hospital, on that particular day when he had me against the wall, I decided to leave the apartment. I got a few of my things, put them into plastic bags and left. I slept in my car for the next several days, coming back to the apartment once in a while during the week when I needed something.

Finally, I conferred with my friend, Mary, about my predicament. She was the first person I told about what was going on in my home. She was shocked as to what I was telling her. She gave me some advice on what I needed to do. I called the Elder Abuse Agency and made my complaint with them. They sent their representative out to talk with me and I was told I needed to go down to family court and file a restraining order against my brother, making sure it is delivered by the sheriff. The restraining order was granted and Glen was not to come within 200 feet of me. He was to leave the apartment until the eviction order was granted. The Sheriff's Department then carried out the restraining order. The Sheriff came to the apartment the next day and told Glen he had to leave, and that he could take some of the clothes that he would need until we went to court again. The other two guys who were living with me also left the following day. I had reclaimed my apartment! Another court date was set where a final decision would be made.

The day of the hearing, I appeared with a friend of mine who had inside knowledge of what was going on in my apartment. Glen showed up with one of the guys that were staying with me along with our cousin, Reverend Manley. Glen came to me before the hearing and wanted to talk. Glen, Reverend Manley, my friend and I went into a room nearby. We discussed the situation and it was agreed that we would ask the court to dismiss the request for the eviction order and Glen would come by the house and pick up the rest of his belongings. He would stay away from me, and my apartment. We went back into the courtroom and when the judge called my case, I stood and told him that I was withdrawing my request; that my brother and I had come to an agreement that he would remove all his belongings and leave my apartment. The judge questioned Glen as to the agreement. When he was satisfied with his answers, he told me he would dismiss the request for eviction and if, in the future I needed to reinstate it, I could.

Several days later Glen came to the apartment to remove the rest of his stuff.

Since I did not want to come into contact with him, I had my housekeeper, who had my keys and the keys to the garage where he also had some of his belongings, meet him. He took his things, thus ending the nightmare. Since then I have had limited contact with Glen and made it clear to him and his wife, Lisa, that I did not want to see them again.

My sixth and youngest brother is Timmy. My mother had him when she was in her late 40's. He was almost 12 pounds when he was born. This was her first legitimate child. All the rest of us were bastards. My mother married Bill Green, Timmy's father, in 1960. He worked for Local Union 89. I was also absent when Timmy grew up. Occasionally I would stop by the house to see him. I noticed as he grew up he kept putting on weight and even to this day he is still overweight. When he was in school, kids would tease him and call him names. I guess this left a permanent scar on his psyche. I had only brief contact with him over the years. After his father died, he began to get into trouble, even more than when Bill was alive. It was rumored that he was selling drugs for my oldest brother and involved in other criminal activities. I remember one time he got in my face and proceeded to lecture me about my lifestyle. I had to put him in his place. Timmy is now doing time in the Federal Correction Facility and I was told he eventually was put into a Federal Witness Program for giving up some of his friends. I just recently received an Easter card from him, and I sent him a card in return. I don't feel I should involve myself with being associated with him at this time in my life. So much has passed and so many things have happened, I just need to be alone without having to worry about his problems. As far as I know, he never married or had any children.

Aunt Bette is one of the most remarkable women I have ever known; complicated, caring, unpredictable, loving and sometimes rude. She is all those things and more. Born in the Deep South, the youngest sister of my mother, she is the pure essence of a strong-willed and independent black woman. She was the youngest of five. She was the one who was there for Sam, Clyde, Sly and me when we were kids. It is she whom I hold dear to my heart for having to bear the burden of taking me back and forth to doctor's appointments because of my childhood polio. She is a huge woman with dark skin and sparkling dark eyes that always show a unique compassion for those less fortunate than she.

However, there were times when I thought she could have shown more compassion for me. She has a dual personality and is a dichotomy. I remember someone told me that she killed her first husband in self-defense. I barely remember her second husband, Jason, but I knew that he was stabbed several times by Aunt Bette during an argument. They were later divorced.

Her third husband, Ladd, was a very gentle man and at one time taught a construction class in which I was enrolled. He helped me get through my Construction Training program. He and my Aunt Bette divorced after several years together, and he died several years later. Her fourth husband, John, was a quiet introverted man who showed a lot of patience and understanding in tolerating the verbal abuse that Aunt Bette leashed upon him; sometimes in private, other times public. It was always the topic of gossip among family and friends, the way she treated Uncle John. But he did not seem to mind her constant tirades and rude behavior. He was a simple man, not prone to grandiose behavior and display. When he married Aunt Bette, he was in the Navy and several years after their marriage he retired. He was always kind to me and I felt a deep and abiding affection for him, especially when he was under attack by one of Aunt Bette's outbursts. This happened when he did not respond to her right away, or when he failed to do something she had asked him to do. Then she would scream. He died July 20, 2004 of natural causes. I made sure to attend his funeral and bid my farewell.

After Uncle John's death, Aunt Bette continued to live in the home where she had lived since the 60's. I sometimes went by to visit her. I usually refrained from calling her because when she gets on the phone she tries her best to monopolize the conversation. She becomes repetitious in matters of which I have no interest. I have kept my distance from her, as well as the rest of my family and relatives, everyone except my nephew, Dimitri.

My brothers and I depended on Aunt Bette. She was always there for us. Since she didn't have children of her own, I guess she looked at us as her own. She always threw parties on Thanksgiving, Christmas and Mother's Day and she would cook all the typical southern dishes, otherwise known as soul food. All our favorites - collard greens, ham hocks, fried Okra, baked chicken, macaroni and cheese, neck bones and rice and sweet potato pies. Those were her most famous dishes. When any one of us needed anything we would go to Aunt Bette; and, in most cases we would get it if we were willing to listen to a long, drawn out lecture telling us how we could have avoided getting into whatever crazy situation we were describing. She never had any real formal education, but she was quite wise from her life experiences and if you listened closely to what she was saying, you could definitely learn something from a very remarkable woman.

When I was a child, she used to care for me, and I have never asked her for any favors. Since she lost her last husband, Uncle John, there are many in the family who think she will not survive much longer because she really loved Uncle John and she is still grieving. Within the last couple of months she has been very ill and living alone in her home. She seems to have deteriorated mentally as well as physically, to the point of no return. Being the remarkable woman that she is, she's still holding her own and there is a possibility that she may outlive all her adopted sons. I think one of the things that keep her going was all those kids Glen had, because they keep running to her house begging for money. She probably realizes that most of them, including my brother, is waiting until she dies so that they can get a hold of all her money. I, for one, have made it clear to her several times that I am too ill to be running out to her house as often as she may want me to. Even if I weren't ill, I don't believe that I would be running out there now, not since I never have in the past. Therefore, it is quite obvious that I am not interested in her money nor am I waiting for her to die.

CHAPTER TEN

The date was March 13, 1981 and I was on a one-year parole. If I completed the one-year parole without any problems with the law, I would be discharged. Upon my release, I went back to stay with my Mom in Emerald Hills. Of course, my stepfather was still there, but I had no other place to go. During those first three weeks I was out I was determined to find myself a job and save some money and get my own place. I was now forty years old and most of my life had been spent behind bars; either in reformatory school when I was in Mississippi, or California State Hospitals, juvenile hall or prison. From the age of twelve I had spent less than five years as a free person. Now it was about time for me to do something for myself. I was determined to make a liar out of the program lieutenant who told me I would be back in prison within six weeks.

The first day I was out of prison I walked from Emerald Hills to downtown San Diego, which is about 2½ miles every day and then back home again. For almost two weeks I filled out applications and checked out new businesses opening downtown. One day while I was walking on First and Broadway, I noticed a new restaurant was opening. It was called Skippy Fish and Chips. I went in and talked to the owner. He had me fill out an application and the next day I was hired as a counter person. Two weeks Later I became the manager.

I worked at Skippy's for the next several months as night shift manager. While working there, I enrolled in San Diego City College and took several courses of law at ECC. I went to school during the day and then worked the night shift. I had no transportation so I had to walk to school, spending several hours there, catch the bus downtown, go to work, work until midnight, clean up the place, go home, get some sleep, wake up in the morning and then back to school again. I had no free time whatsoever. After I was on the job for about two months I had saved enough money to get my own place.

It was a small studio apartment right across from San Diego City College on 14th and B Streets. When I first moved to my studio I didn't have any furniture. Each week I bought some, little by little. Most of it was purchased at secondhand or thrift stores. Eventually my apartment was furnished. I had a bed, a little furniture in the livingroom and a few dishes. I was content with what I had. I had a roof over my head. I was employed. I was going to college to pursue my dreams and to keep myself from going back to prison. Each time I thought about what the lieutenant told me, I became more motivated than ever. I was determined to succeed. My job at Skippy's ended when I hired a friend of mine who I didn't know was selling drugs to his friends in the restaurant. When the owner found out he talked to me about it and due to the fact that I had recommended him for the job, I decided to quit when my friend was fired.

After quitting my job at Skippy's Fish and Chips Restaurant, I could not find another job right away. Being an ex-felon, it was not easy for me to find employment. I had some money and my rent was paid for the month, but I needed to find another job. For the next two months I searched relentlessly for employment. Eventually my money ran out. I refused to ask my relatives for help and I was determined not to return back to prison by doing something stupid. I kept remembering what I had told the prison lieutenant when he told me that I was going to be released from CMC East. He said, "You will be back in two weeks!" And I told him not to hold his breath, I wouldn't be! I ended up in the streets sleeping in Balboa Park for several weeks. I had a little corner northeast of Marston Point. It was approximately 300 ft from the old Aerospace Museum where I once had helped restore the famous art pieces that adorned the building that was built for the World's Fair in San Diego in the early 1900's.

The weeks that I slept in Balboa Park underneath a large giant eucalyptus tree, was perhaps the worst time of my life. Fortunately, it was summer because the only thing that I had to keep me warm at night was a long leather coat, which I had bought for $300 in Los Angeles. The other clothes I had were in a duffel bag that had been stolen while I slept one night. Each morning as I awoke I felt dirty. I could not brush my teeth, wash my face, comb my hair or take a shower for days. I was always hungry and I stole food from stores around the park area. I hustled enough money in the park to buy a meal. Finally I ran into a friend who gave me some money to get a room for a few nights. I bought some used clothes and went job-hunting the next day. I soon found employment in a convalescent hospital on Fourth Avenue in Hillcrest.

I worked as a nurse's assistant, taking vital signs, feeding patients, changing diapers and pads, making beds and giving showers. I was required to take a class to become certified by the State of California. Certification was mandatory for me to continue to work at the hospital. I finished the class, received my state certification and now I was a CNA, a certified nurses assistant. I received a CNA gold pin, which I still have. I remember the day when the supervising nurse pinned the pin on my uniform and I made a vow to myself that I would never again be homeless. Mercy Rehabilitation and Convalescent Hospital gave me inspiration and determination to better myself and elevate myself to a higher level. After working as a CNA for almost a year, I was asked to become a medical records clerk. My charge nurse told me that I was chosen because of my excellent work as a CNA and because of my writing and charting abilities. Accuracy in charting of a patient was one of the prerequisites of a good nurse and one of the hallmarks for a good medical records clerk. Within months working on the second floor of the skill facility as a medical records clerk, I practically ran the entire floor. My abilities to decipher and translate doctor's orders, arrange patient transportation, audit, do the licensed nurses notes, document orders for patient's lab work, complete admission and transfer orders and keep an accurate census brought me praise and honor from my supervisors. It also brought me a few enemies.

There were those who did not like that I had as much as, and often more than, the authority than some of the licensed nurses. Some of them did not like how I audited the nurses notes and corrected errors in the diagnosis summary. There were some CNA's who disliked me for reporting their poor charting in the patients' charts. Such accuracy in ordering patient care was necessary, not only for professionalism, but to keep the hospital in good standing with the State of California and in keeping their requirements. I was awarded a special citation for helping the hospital pass the rigorous state inspection exam. That special citation still hangs on my wall. After about two years as a medical records clerk, I voluntarily resigned when I was accused of being rude to a family member of one of the patients. Later I was told that one of the CNA's, one who I had persistently corrected this patient notes, was determined to get me fired. I accepted this defeat and moved on.

While I was still at Mercy, James Brown came to the hospital and applied for a Medical Records position. He was hired and I was assigned to train him. He was a very apt and intelligent individual - young, tall and very good looking. It took me only two weeks to train him and they assigned him to another floor where he steadily made progress as a medical records clerk. We became very close friends and I teased him a lot about his name, James Brown, a name he shared with the famous singer. When I left Mercy, he was still there. I often ran into him at restaurants or coffee shops and he always told the people he was with how I helped him get his position and how I trained him. According to him, I was responsible for the success in his career. Recently I ran into him at the Norman Heights Spring Festival and he was with a of couple friends. He was very happy to see me. He told me that he had advanced in his career and that he was now working for Sharp Cabrillo Hospital in the medical records department. He said he was making more money, and he thanked me over, and over, and over again for helping him, telling his two friends that I was responsible for where he is today. That comment made me feel pretty good.

Since I had taken several law courses earlier and had enough experience to be a paralegal, I decided to pursue this career.

First I enrolled in a paralegal course at Kelsey Jenny College while I was working as a private duty CNA for a nursing agency. I did not finish the program but was proficient enough to become an independent paralegal.

During this time, I had met a young man named Cedric Arey. He was an avowed Muslim, 24 years old and very handsome. He had taken the paralegal course at Kelsey Jenny College with me. His knowledge of the law was as profound as mine so we decided to operate a paralegal business together. He also moved in with me to save money. Although he knew of my sexual proclivities our relationship was strictly business. We did very well for the first year but when I became ill, I eventually had to quit. Even though I never saw him again, I am sure he made a great success out of his career.

Right after Cedric left my house I took out a loan of $5,000 from a credit card company who was offering a low interest rate. I took the money and opened up a florist shop on the corner of Fourth and University Avenue. I sublet the space inside a coffee shop called Cafe Fiore. It was a very popular place for straights and gays. I named my flower shop "Flowers Plus". A few months earlier I had taken a floral arrangement course at a school in Kensington and I became experienced in designing and arrangement. The following Valentine's Day I made over $5,000 selling bouquets of roses and unique Valentine arrangements. One day Lisa Lake (from Channel 10 news) came into my shop and bought a floral design for her mother. I met many interesting people while selling flowers and I also did floral arrangements for several businesses in the neighborhood. I made small, unique floral arrangements as centerpieces for the Taste of Thai Restaurant and Little Tokyo Restaurant. During the two years I operated my flower shop, I earned the nickname as Mayor of Hillcrest. Finally, when the owner of the coffee shop lost his lease, I had to move my shop. I rented a temporary place on Fifth Avenue, about four blocks from where I had been. The location was not nearly as profitable, so after a few months I gave up the floral business and went into landscaping.

After this experience, I was hired by the County Mental Health Department as a mental health worker. I found my work with the department very interesting and rewarding. I was able to help people with their problems and conduct counseling groups for patients. My job was to admit patients, document the patient's history, chart their behavior, take vital signs and report any unusual behavior to the charge nurse or the doctor. I got along well with other staff members. Many people referred to me as Dr. Brown. It seemed that due to the fact that my name is David Ray Brown, the "DR" stuck in people's minds as "doctor", so they called me Dr. Brown. Many of the patients were violent, schizoid, and bi-polar and many of them were admitted under the influence of drugs. There were numerous occasions that we had to take someone down and strap them into their bed to keep them from hurting other staff members or themselves. This could be a dangerous job. You had to keep your eyes open at all times because someone could come up behind you, pluck you one and you were out on the floor. It always seemed to me that I had a way with people with mental problems. I could defuse situations that seemed to be on the verge of getting out hand where somebody might get hurt.

One incident occurred when one of my patients was released from the ward and I was just getting off work. I got to the bus stop at UCSD Hospital. He was there standing at the bus stop. He did not see me. The bus pulled up. He got onto the bus and I came on the bus behind him. As I was paying my fare there was a lot of noise coming from the back of the bus. Evidently he had gotten into an argument with one of the passengers. He was threatening someone and then two or three other people got involved. The bus driver got up to investigate. Then I realized that the person responsible was my ex-patient. I immediately intervened in the situation and finally calmed the patient down. I got him quiet and sitting in his seat. When he got off the bus, I hadn't reached my destination. When I did the driver thanked me for diverting the situation. I explained to him that I worked with these people and I was happy I could be there to help.

Also while working at CMH, I discovered corruption by some of the nurses and officials of the County Mental Health Department. I wasn't the only one who noticed it; there was another mental health worker who also noticed indiscretions in some of the reporting on the patients. We discovered that there were people listed on the payroll who were not working there. There was flagrant abuse of some of the patients. On several occasions I witnessed patients who were strapped to the bed and could not defend themselves. The mental health workers were beating the patients. When I raised objections to the beatings, I was told to mind my own business. Being the type of person I am, I could not overlook the fact that there was physical abuse of a patient. I took my complaints outside the department and made sworn statements. An investigation was begun to see if there were any truth to the allegations. It was determined that there was padding of the books by a couple of the head nurses. Some of the mental health workers whose names appeared on the schedule were not working but getting paid. Also, the investigation into the abuse of the patients was continued to determine how much abuse was going on.

During this period a young man, perhaps 15 or 16 years old was admitted on my ward. He had a lot of mental problems and one of his major problems was addiction. He lived with his Mom in La Mesa. She was single and from his initial admitting report, she was unable to control or take care of him. He was assigned to me as part of my caseload. I tried to talk to him and reason with him as to how to create a better situation in his life and to help him understand his behavior. There were times during the counseling that he tried to talk me into bring him some drugs and, of course, I refused. Finally, the doctor released him. He came to me and asked me if I would drop him off downtown. He had no money to catch a bus, so I agreed.

On the way downtown we struck up a conversation. He told me he didn't want to go back home and stay with his mom and that he had no other place to go. I told him that his release form stated that he must go back and stay with his mother because he was underage. Finally I convinced him to go home by promising that I would keep in contact and call him the next day to make sure he was okay. I dropped him off downtown and the next day I called his home. He answered the phone and I agreed to talk to him again. We had made arrangements to meet at a coffee shop on Broadway three days later. Somehow in that short time, someone had apparently set up a situation between this young man and me.

They found out about my past history with the police and probably because of my statements against some of the staff members at CMH, there appeared to be a setup to discredit me. So when I met with the young man at the coffee shop, he was wired. The conversation I had with him, I know for a fact, was not incriminating. But the police arrested me the same day and accused me of trying to solicit the kid into a sexual relationship. They said they had it on tape. I told them it was not so. They said the kid was willing to testify against me in a court of law. Due to my past convictions, I would not have a chance to defend myself in a court of law. They told me if I were convicted of this crime, I would never see daylight again. I would have been convicted three times of a felony.

I consulted with my attorney. He said that he had heard the tape and the tape was indecipherable. And of course there was nothing on it that was incriminating. However, he said, with my past history and my past convictions, I would be taking a chance. By knowing what happened in the last case of being charged with a crime against nature, I probably wouldn't stand a chance with a jury. I had no faith in the judicial system. I believed that if the police had had a case against me, they would never have made a deal. They would rather see me off the streets. So due to the lack of evidence and my innocence in any wrong doing in this case, they made a deal with me. If I pled guilty to a misdemeanor of solicitation, they would give me one year in the County Jail. I had to think about it. Here I was again in a Catch 22 situation. Should I plead innocent, go to trial and take a chance with another all-white jury or end up the rest of my life in prison? The other option was to take the deal and spend a year in jail. That's a hard choice to make when you're innocent. But I was determined not to go back to prison and I was not willing to take a chance with the judicial system again. So I took the plea and spent one year in a County camp and was released.

Also in 1981, after being paroled from prison, I attended San Diego City College. I went to ECC and took pre-law classes. While there, I became involved with the student body and became Vice President. My grades were excellent, with a 4.0 grade average in all my classes. When I ran for the Vice President of the student body, there was a young man who was much more popular than I who was also running for this office. At the time, the President was a woman. She had promised each of us that she was stepping down as president, and whoever won would become President of the student body. It was presumed, due to the fact that everybody knew I was gay that the young man, who was very popular among all the black students, would win. However, there was a sizeable amount of Vietnamese students, so I decided that I would reach out to them and also to the white students. I went to the classes where the majority of students were Vietnamese and I talked to them (through interpreters), trying to garner their vote. That was one of my strategies to beat the young man in the election. He was really mad, too.

After I won the Vice President position, the President refused to step down. It was rumored that ECC could not have a gay as its President. I quietly accepted the fact that it wasn't time for me to be President of the student body. During my tenure as Vice President, I organized different student activities, such as having special symposiums and lectures given by noted leaders in the San Diego Community, such as judges, lawyers, and politicians. They would come to the school and students had a chance to ask questions. It was well accepted by the student body and I was commended for my efforts in bringing these people to the college. I was a member of the Disciplinary Committee and whenever the students got into trouble, they were referred to me and I would submit their problems to the committee. I tried to resolve whatever infraction made by the student, being very concerned about not having the student kicked out of school. If the student were found guilty, instead of termination his punishment would be extra responsibilities or suspension for a couple of days. This would enable the student to continue his/her education.

Many of these students went on to further their education and had great careers after that. After a while, I became so well known at ECC that whenever there was a problem with staff or the students, they would call me and ask how to handle the situation. During my second year at ECC and as vice president, I became quite ill and had to leave school without having the necessary credits to get my degree. I knew I was sick but I didn't realize what the problem was. I had weakness, and shortness of breath. I had night sweats, headaches, and I was losing my appetite. I decided to volunteer at the San Diego Aids Foundation, which was located on Fourth Avenue in Hillcrest.

Probably somewhere in my mind, knowing what I did about AIDS and its symptoms, I knew I had the HIV virus. It was only in 1983, that I decided to take the test, and my test came back positive. I was not told what to do. I was not given any advice. I left the clinic and went home, where I spent the next several weeks in my apartment. The only time I even got up was to go to the bathroom or the kitchen. Nobody called and no one came by. After six weeks, I decided it was time for me to get out of bed and see what I could do for myself. My rent was due and I had no food left, so I sought help. I went to the San Diego

Aids Foundation where they helped me obtain financial aid and then also hooked me up with the food bank. At the time, I was also working as a CNA. There were several other people at the rehab center whom I found later was also HIV positive. A couple of those people passed away while I was working there. I went to their funerals. I just knew that I was going to die soon! I tried to continue to do my best as a nurse assistant and I finally was moved up to the position of medical records clerk. Finally, after working probably a year and a half, I succumbed to all the depression I was going through, and had to quit.

I finally consulted a doctor, Dr. Daniel Pierce, who treated me. He wanted to put me on AZT, which at the time was the best-known drug to fight HIV. I had a lot of knowledge of the drug, and I knew that some of my friends at the aids foundation were taking it. Many of them were passing away right and left. Just dying. So I decided not to take the AZT drug.

Nine years went by. I was still seeing Dr. Pierce and still not taking the drug. If I had something wrong, I would go to him and he would give me an antibiotic or some other treatment. I also went every month for regular checkups. In 1992, they began to come out with new types of drugs, which they called cocktails, because it was a mixture of 3 or 4 drugs. It was only in 1996 that I decided to try one of the cocktails. They consisted of Viracept, Zerit, and Apevert. They later combined Zerit and Apevert and it is now called Truvada. This seemed to help. It seemed a lot of problems I was having such as weakness, diarrhea, loss of appetite and weight loss begun to improve. In the previous thirteen years, I had numerous problems and still had not been diagnosed as an AIDS case.

During the early 80's I lived in El Cajon City where I rented a small cottage on Mollison and Main Streets. I placed an ad on the bulletin board in a peep show on 54th and University Avenue, seeking a companion.

It read something basic like -- "Single guy seeks handsome single guy". I received several responses. There was one guy named Ted. I agreed to meet him at a Denny's Restaurant in Mission Valley. Ted was an older gentleman about 15 years older than me. He was very articulate and spoke in a very intelligent manner. I found out that he spoke several languages, lived in Normal Heights, raised rare parrots and was a contributing writer for various magazines specializing in rare parrots. He lived with his lover of 28 years, Gene. At the time I met him, Gene had contracted the HIV virus, but Ted had tested negative. Apparently, for the last few years before I met him, he and Gene had begun to have an open relationship.

Ted and Gene would come to visit with me often. We would often argue about politics and social issues. Ted was very opinionated and so was I. There was a personality conflict between us. There were times we would get into heated discussions and stop speaking to each other for weeks, sometimes months. In 2004 we had a severe falling out with each other and I told him I did not want to see him anymore and we have not spoken since.

At the beginning of our friendship, Ted and I were sometimes intimate and enjoyed each other's company. But as time went by, we drifted apart in terms of an intimate relationship. However, we did remain friends. I would visit him quite often in his Clairemont home. At this point, Gene had passed away from AIDS related complications in the late 1980's. After that, our relationship became strained. Ted had found a new friend, Howard, who, interestingly, had almost the identical last name as Gene.

Its really difficult to understand Ted and the difficulties I had in dealing with his arrogant and superior attitude. He was an avowed atheist who at one time was married and had a son. His homosexual fantasies began to materialize after he divorced his wife. His number one objective is to satisfy his own sexual desires without any consideration for his partner. At one time, he had thousands of photos of young black naked boys and men from all over the world, that filled over 100 scrapbooks; especially men from South America. Since he spoke several languages, including French and Spanish, and had traveled the world extensively as a writer on rare parrots, he was always meeting young men and taking their pictures. He would often tell me lurid stories about young Jamaicans, Puerto Ricans and Brazilians with whom he had had affairs.

Ted also served many years in the military and was mentioned in a book by a friend who was in the service with him. I sometimes ask myself how I lasted for so many years as his friend. I guess because I really cared for him and because he was intellectual and knowledgeable; I learned a great deal from him. Ted had a great passion for black men and I have never known him to be involved with anyone of any other race. There were many times when we would be out together, riding in his car, having dinner in a restaurant, when he would see a very handsome, well-built young black guy and make sexual comments about that person. Sometimes he would stare at a guy so hard that it embarrassed me.

When Gene died in the early 1980's, Ted called me every week, crying on the telephone and telling me how much he loved Gene and how much he missed him. I was very sympathetic toward him and told him that he had to forget about the past and start living his own life again.

El Cajon was a town with a diverse population; there were rednecks, gang members, bigots and misfits. I found myself living between a bigot and a couple of rednecks. For two years, I had a running battle with the cottage on my left and the one on my right. There was one time I remember the rednecks in the cottage to my right and I got into a heated argument about trespassing on my lawn. The guy picked up a rake and threatened me with it. I grabbed the rake while he still had it in his hand, took it away and started beating him with it. By this time there were several witnesses. When the police arrived I explained to them that the guy threatened me with the rake and I was defending myself. No one went to jail that day. The police seemed to diffuse the situation and a couple of months after that I moved back to San Diego.

While I still lived in El Cajon, there was one young man that I was intimately involved with who lived a couple of blocks from me. He spent a great deal of time at my cottage. His mother and I worked at the same convalescent hospital and that's how I met him. He was young, very handsome and had an insatiable passion when it came to sex. When we were together he seemed to enjoy himself and there were times when I could not get rid of him. But when I did, he would return home where he lived with his mother. The following day, however, he would be back at my door again. One day he left my cottage, went home and about two hours later I heard sirens and saw a fire truck going down Mollison Street in front of my house. The following day I was called by his mother who told me that Mark had come home that evening, was laying on the sofa watching the TV with a cigarette in his hand, when he fell asleep. The apartment had caught on fire and Mark had burned to death. That same day I purchased a newspaper, which had the complete story on the front page. I cut it out and saved it.

CHAPTER ELEVEN

In 1989 I worked as a volunteer for Being Alive HIV Organization. I was selected to represent Being Alive for the March on Washington, DC. The purpose of the March was to make the government aware of the seriousness of the AIDS epidemic throughout the United States. When I was selected to be a representative to go to Washington I could not make up my mind whether to go or not, due to the fact that I had never flown in an airplane and I had a fear of flying. I decided to go anyway. A couple of other people went including Ann MacCarty, another volunteer who was in a wheelchair because she was paralyzed, Andy Malone, and myself. We were the representatives for Being Alive. When we arrived in Washington, DC, it was very chilly and a very strange place for me. I was fascinated by all of the monuments and the White House, the Capitol Building and especially the United States Supreme Court Building. The next day we met on the Mall and there were thousands and thousands of people stretched from the Washington to Lincoln Monuments.

The AIDS quilt was spread out and covered half of the Mall. There were names of individuals who had died of AIDS from all over the United States. It was a beautiful quilt, yet it was very painful for me to look at the names of people who had died from this terrible disease, knowing that I, too, might soon die. The next day we went out sightseeing throughout the capitol. We had a choice as to whether to visit the White House, for which we had to get special permission, or the US Supreme Court Bldg, which also called for special permission. I chose the Supreme Court Building probably because I have always been fascinated with the law and the judicial system.

I also visited the Vietnam Monument. I was flabbergasted by all the names that were listed on the granite wall, knowing that these were young men who had lost their lives in an unjust war. I also visited the US Capitol and looked into some of the Senate and Representatives rooms and walked down the ornate halls and across the red carpet. Then I went to the rotunda and I stood there for several minutes remembering the assassination of John F. Kennedy and seeing his casket lying in state there. I also visited the huge United States library located in the

Capitol and the Smithsonian Institute. After several days of visiting all these famous places and monuments I began to be very happy that I had made the trip. On the day we were supposed to return home to San Diego, I was anxious all over again of flying back. I remember as we neared Lindbergh Field coming over Balboa Park, we hit wind turbulence and the plane began to rattle a little bit and I was really afraid again. I thought we would never land safely. When the plane finally touched down, I was so happy that I vowed never again to get on another plane!

I continued to volunteer for Being Alive for the next ten years. During the last two years with them, I became a paid staff member. I was Peer Advocate Recruiter Specialist. My job was to recruit and train, and during the next couple of years I trained many peer advocates for Being Alive. Peer Advocate is a helper for individuals who come for help, information, medications, etc. All Peer Advocate Recruiters and Trainers had to be positive for HIV or AIDS.

During the period that I served as a member of the staff for Being Alive, I created several programs to help people who had HIV and AIDS diagnosis. One of the programs was home and hospital visits where one or two peer advocates would visit people with HIV and AIDS in their homes, or go to the hospital and visit them and carry them flowers. The other program was providing them with a light breakfast in the morning from Monday to Friday and I managed this by asking restaurants, cafes and coffee shops in Hillcrest for food donations. The City Delicatessen, which is still on Sixth and University Avenue, donated eighty percent of the food for these breakfast visits. It was here that I first met Jess San Rogue and Elmer (Al) F. Bisarra who had come to Being Alive with an organization called APICAP - (Asian Pacific Islander Community Aids Project. They were just starting out with this new Asian HIV/AIDS Organization and Being Alive gave them space for an office. I worked closely with Jess and Al in helping them setup their organization, which led to a long and abiding friendship. I am still a member of APICAP.

After my release from CMC East in 1981, I became dedicated to my commitment to helping others, especially the youth. I was very cautious as to how I did my volunteer work with young people because of my past experience, which led to my arrest and conviction of a crime that I didn't commit. One of the ways I worked on behalf of young people was going to high schools to speak on HIV and AIDS, explaining to them how to use a condom. One of the first speaking engagements I gave was a lecture to UCSD Law Class on Life in Prison and Juvenile Delinquency and the Law. I spoke about my life in prison and as a juvenile. I talked about the justice system and the double standards of the law as it is applied to the rich and the poor. My lecture was well received by the law students. There was a question and answer period afterward and there were many questions, I soon had to cut it off for lack of time. My next speaking engagement was at an all girls' Catholic school. The students ranged from the ages of 12 to 16. There were three speakers that day including myself; all three of us were HIV positive. We talked about HIV and AIDS and the need to use condoms and practice safe sex. Such a lecture about sex and condoms before an all girl Catholic school was unheard of before that time. When the speaking engagement was over both school officials and the students commended us for our presentation. This speaking engagement was under the auspices of "Being Alive", an HIV organization.

There were many questions by the girls as to how to use a condom, how HIV is transmitted and how long each one of us had lived with HIV or AIDS. We explained to them in general terms about the use of condoms, being more specific about the transmission of HIV and AIDS. Each one of us told how long we had been living with the disease.

After that speaking engagement I became a member of an organization called Positively Speaking. This organization's main purpose and goal was to train each speaking member, teaching them the necessary skills and tools to be able to talk to High School students and other youth organizations about HIV and AIDS. I had the opportunity to speak at several high schools, sometimes with a couple of other speakers and sometimes alone. I found that students were very receptive to the information we gave them. They were curious to know about the transmission of HIV and AIDS. Many of them wanted to know if HIV and AIDS was mainly a gay disease and what did we think about men having sex with men and whether such a lifestyle promotes these diseases. We also explained to them about transmission through the use of drugs as well as practicing safe sex. My first thought of the many questions the students asked were that they were very interested in having the information about HIV and AIDS so that they may be better equipped to prevent themselves from catching the disease.

While volunteering as a staff member of Being Alive, I continued to go on speaking engagements and giving lectures, which created a greater awareness of how the HIV virus is transmitted and the importance of using condoms and practicing safe sex. From 1983 to 1996, I spoke at more than 25 speaking engagements.

Helping others understand the causes of this disease seemed to give me a purpose in life and made me feel good about myself. Within those thirteen years, I reached out to many people in many ways, including the homeless and the elderly. The homeless I would help acquire shelter and give them money for food sometimes. I assisted the elderly with chores and running errands for them. It was another way for me to show how much I was blessed by God, of still being alive and that He had protected me through all the trials and tribulations of my past life.

CHAPTER TWELVE

Years later after Bill passed away and the death of my mother, I was told that there was a will that gave my oldest brother 55% of the estate. I was to get 5%. Carl was to get 15%, Clyde was to get 10%, Glen was to get 5%, Sly was to get 5% and Timmy was to get 5%. I was very surprised as to who got what from my mother's estate, especially my oldest brother getting 55%, more than anyone else. For the last two years of my mother's life, various members of the family told me, that my oldest brother, Sam, had influenced my mother to change her will. During these two years also, my mother had suffered from Alzheimer's disease, which perhaps made her vulnerable to the influence of my oldest brother. I had no knowledge of my mother's medical condition and when I questioned my brother about it he simply evaded the issue. I decided not to push it any further due to the fact that there were some questions as to whether the house would be sold or kept in the family. Since I didn't know how much more time I was going to live due to my own illness, I wanted the house sold. I wanted to bury the memories that had haunted me all my life from the abuse of my stepfather, and to the hateful relationship between my mother and I. After I talked my brother into selling the house and we agreed, I decided this was in the best interest of all of us so we could get this situation behind us.

When the house was put up for sale we had it cleaned and fumigated. The day the house was fumigated, Carl took Clyde over to Aunt Bette's house to stay there until the fumigation was over. But due to Clyde's drinking problem, Aunt Bette told Carl to get Clyde a motel room, as was previously agreed to. The house was fumigated that day and by evening, I was told by Aunt Bette, that Carl dropped Clyde off down the hill from our home at a liquor store. Evidently, Clyde got drunk that night and he went back to the house, pulled up the tarp, went thru a back window, went into his room and fell asleep. He must have at some point realized he was in danger, got up out of the bed, made an attempt to get to the front door and fell by the hot water heater in the hallway. That's where they found him the next day. Dead! I was unaware that all this had happened. But knowing Clyde as I did and being a mama's boy, I could understand why he wanted to go back home and go to sleep in his own room. This is something he had been doing most of his life. Living with mama. I don't think he ever got over the death of our mother. Later I questioned Carl about how he handled the situation and told him that he was just as guilty of Clyde's death as the poison that flowed through his body. He should have known not to leave Clyde alone and made sure he had a place to stay away from home safely until the fumigation was completed. I was not the only one to blame Carl for the death of Clyde. Most of the family concurred on this.

The house was sold for $250,000; debts were paid from the proceeds. My oldest brother received $144,000 and I received my $10,000. Then I broke all ties with my brothers and close family friends.

My brother, Carl, was my brother Clyde's conservator. Clyde was an alcoholic. He received approximately $1200 each month from the Federal Government for serving in the Vietnam War. He served approximately two and a half years in Vietnam before he was discharged from the Navy after being diagnosed with an acute case of shell shock. After returning home from the war, Clyde was never the same. He spent every penny that he got from the Federal Government on drugs and alcohol. Finally we had to step in and take control of his finances. His first conservator was my mother. She controlled his finances, made sure he had a place to stay and gave him an allotment every week to purchase his alcohol and cigarettes. After mama became ill and could no longer administrate his finances, it was turned over to my brother, Carl. There are still some questions as to what happened to most of Clyde's money before and after he died. There was evidence that there was a substantial amount of money in Clyde's name at Bank of America. When Carl was questioned about the whereabouts of all the money, he could not justify or account for it.

In the late 1990's I contracted pneumocystis pneumonia, which meant that I had gone from HIV to an AIDS diagnosis. It was late one afternoon I was alone in my apartment when I lost consciousness. I seemed to know where I was at certain times or had a feeling that I still existed, but I knew something was wrong. I remember falling off the bed onto the floor when I began to reach for something that I could not remember at the time. Then it appeared somewhere deep in my subconscious mind that there was a knocking sound. I could not tell what the sound was, but still I went toward it. I can't remember how I got to the front door, but somehow without my knowledge, I managed to open it. I heard voices. Then time lapsed and I heard a siren. I felt myself moving. Then I went unconscious again. I don't remember anything until I woke up in a hospital bed the next day.

For the second time in my life I had all kinds of tubes running out of me. When I became conscious and I looked around the hospital room there was no one there but me. I surveyed the room, saw the intravenous drip running, there was an oxygen tank in the corner of the room and I looked on the side of the bed and realized I had a catheter. Then I reached for the signal button. I pushed the button, a nurse came and she told me that I was at Mercy Hospital, and that three friends had brought me there. It was Jess, Al and Maria Galleta. I also later found out that they had come by my house to check on me because they hadn't seen me for several days and it was very uncommon for me not to be seen at Being Alive nearly every day.

They had never been to my apartment before. Actually, they didn't even know where I lived. Because of their concern for me, they went to my supervisor at Being Alive and told him about their worries. He gave them my telephone number and address. They said they tried to call me but they couldn't get anyone to answer the telephone. They then decided to come by. They said when they went to the door and knocked, knocking several times before the door opened, they found me delirious and in a mess. They immediately called 911 and while they were waiting for them, they took me to the bathroom and bathed me and put me in clean clothes. Before I was discharged from the hospital, the doctor told them that if they had not come by when they did, I would have been dead by the next morning. I never would have survived through the night. The first few days I was at the hospital I got up out of my bed for the first time and went to the bathroom on my own. I looked into the mirror. I was startled by what I saw! After several days of doing exercises I began to see some improvement. My face had sunken in. The image looking back at me looked like a skeleton. I had lost all the meat in my face and you could see nothing but bones. I was extremely shaken by what I saw and I just knew that

I was not going to make it. But somehow over the next couple days I decided that I wasn't going to die. I thought to myself that God was with me as he always had been and this was not my time to die. I began to get up every morning for the next week and then they discharged me. Most of my weight had returned, my face had filled in and I felt pretty good. I returned back to Being Alive a couple of weeks later and resumed my volunteer work. My friends were surprised to see me and at how fast I had bounced back from my ordeal. At this stage I was on disability, as well as a paid staff member of Being Alive.

In 1996, I moved from my studio apartment on Florida Street where I had contracted pneumonia, and moved to Hamilton Street where I presently reside. I met Eddie Cong about a year later while I was doing some volunteer work at the Neil Goods Center, which is a homeless shelter organization. I answered the telephone, passed out meals to the homeless, answered questions and assisted them in finding employment. Eddie was one of the homeless clients that came in every day to take a shower and to get his meals.

When I first met Eddie, in 2000, he was into the Rastafarian Cult. He had long dreadlocks and facial hair. He wore a skullcap of some kind on his head. Eddie was about twenty years younger than me. My first impression of him was that he looked weird. We talked several times before I decided to trust him in my house. We talked about his unusual dress and appearance and why he wanted to be a "Rasta Man". After a lot of discussion and extensive talks about his appearance, he finally decided to give up his lifestyle and come and stay with me. That was my mandate. After he had shaved, cut his hair and began to dress differently, he was. very handsome and had a lot of sex appeal. His knowledge of computers and electronics was phenomenal. He had an uncle, whom I had met several times, who owned a Judo school on Fifth Avenue, who also possessed a black belt. Eddie had been trained by his uncle in Judo and was very good at self-defense. Eddie and I became emotionally involved with each other over the next two years. Off and on he would get into trouble with the law due to his bipolar and manic depression illness. During the time of his troubles with the law, I stood by him and supported him. Eddie assisted me in my landscaping business, making flyers, doing inventory, purchasing supplies and simple manual labor.

He was always jolly, happy and outgoing. He was very intelligent. But later on, I started to see a different side of him. I began to realize that he was bipolar. Because of my previous experience of working with schizophrenics, bipolars and other mental patients, I knew the symptoms. I could always tell when he was going through one of these phases because he would begin to become agitated and talking nonsense. I would ask him if he had been taking his medication and he would answer that he hadn't. I continued to question him and demand that he take his medication. During this period of our relationship, which spanned the next three years, he would do odd things. Such as the first time he disappeared for two or three days. When he finally did call, he told me he was in jail and that he had stolen something. He did some time for the theft and then returned back to the house. He would stay for a brief period and then get in trouble again.

This went on until around 2002 when one day I went out to Ocean Beach with him to visit my friend, Mr. VJ Ninteman. Usually Eddie would go with me to visit VJ, but he was agitated this day. I had noticed the change in him early. He did not want to go into the house so I decided to go in by myself. Just before we got to VJ's house, and I had picked Eddie up at the Probation Department, I had gone by the bank and got a thousand dollars worth of traveler's checks. I stuck the checks in a compartment in the middle divider between the seats of the truck. I was in the house talking to VJ for about fifteen minutes when I decided to go back to the truck to check on Eddie and he was gone! Something told me to look in the compartment and the traveler checks were gone. This happened on a Sunday and I was not able to call the bank until Monday. When Monday morning came I called the bank and was instructed as to what to do to have the traveler's checks cancelled.

They picked Eddie up several days later and he is still in jail for this offense. I was refunded all my money. He continued to write me from jail. His parole officer called me and informed me that he was getting out soon and asked if I wanted him to come back and stay with me. No, I did not. I also told the parole officer that he had been writing me, but I had not answered any of his letters since he's been in jail. I had no intention of having a relationship with him again. Eddie wore on me. He is a remarkable young man and I still love him. He is serving time at the George C. Bailey Facility in Otay Mesa. Eddie remains close to my heart and probably always will.

I met William Brown in 2000 also at the Neil Good Homeless Center and I invited him home. We started an open relationship whereas he would come to the house and spend two or three nights and then he'd be gone for maybe a week or so. He would call me and we would go out to dinner or to a movie. It was not actually a permanent situation. You might say we were just very close friends who had a lot in common. There were times that he would work for me in my business doing landscaping projects and other times I was helping him with some of his personal family problems. He was a very sweet, intelligent individual, approximately twenty years younger than me.

His only hang up, as far as I was could tell, was his drinking problem. When he was not drinking, he was a caring, open-minded and outgoing person. But when he drank, his whole personality changed. He became moody and distrustful. Also, when he went to nightclubs he'd usually go without me; he would go to straight nightclubs and I wasn't interested. During these escapades he would usually get into a fight and the first person he would call would be me to bail him out. I guess you might say that I was emotionally attached to William Brown because we did share a great deal in common, notwithstanding the fact that we shared the same last name. As kids growing up we both were abused and came from dysfunctional families.

One day in 2003, William came to me and said that he wanted to return home to the East Coast to be with his son who, at this time, was around fourteen years old. He wanted to become part of his son's life. William had a difficult time accepting his sexuality and often would pretend to be straight. I told him it was all right to leave and thought it was a good idea that he go back and help raise his son. The night before he left he spent the night with me and left the next morning. Since he's been gone, I have received several letters from him but he never mentions that he will be coming back soon. I hope that someday he will come back to San Diego.

CHAPTER THIRTEEN

One day in 2004, as I was driving west on University Avenue on my way to K-Mart on 54th Street, I noticed a young man walking along on the sidewalk. I slowed down to get a better look at him. I noticed that he was very feminine and he appeared to be gay. I decided to stop and check him out. I pulled ahead of him about a hundred feet, pulled my car to the curb and parked. I waited until he walked up close to the car and I blew my horn. He stopped and came to the window on the passenger's side. I asked him where he was going and could I give him a ride. He said he was going to a friend's house just off of University Avenue. I told him I would take him there. He got into the car and we drove off. He told me that his name was Aphram and that he was 20 years old. I introduced myself. I asked him where he was from and he said he was from Ethiopia. I asked him if he had a job and he said no, that he was looking for work. I asked him if he had ever done any landscaping. He wanted to know what landscaping was. I explained it to him.

By the time we reached his friend's house I had told him that I needed some help with my landscaping business. I would teach him everything he needed to know. After we pulled up to his friend's home I gave him my cell and home phone numbers. I asked him to call me later. Later that evening Aphram called me and I invited him over to the house. He had no transportation so he gave me his address and I went to pick him up. I brought him home and we talked for a couple of hours. I learned that he lived with his sister who had been in this country for approximately three years and he only for about a year. They had both come to America from Ethiopia via Nairobi. They had left two brothers, one sister and their father behind. Their mother had died several years before. Aphram spoke very little English; he said his sister spoke more. For the next several weeks Aphram helped me on different landscaping projects. I noticed that he was a quick learner and was enthusiastic about what he was doing. I had trouble understanding him sometimes due to his little English, but we managed to communicate whenever it was necessary.

One day after work we were at my house and I confronted him about his sexuality. He told me that he was not gay and that boys and men in his country always had close relationships. Most of them had feminine characteristics and would hug each other upon approaching, sometimes holding hands. It was never considered abnormal or unusual. I didn't pursue the subject any further. A few days later we were at the house and I approached him again about his sexuality. I explained to him that I was gay and was very interested in having a relationship with him. He did not seem repulsed about my asking him. I noticed, however, there were some signs of evasiveness. So again, I dropped the subject. For the next several weeks I became very close to him and found myself becoming emotionally involved with him. So I decided to back away. One reason was he did not seem interested and my feelings for him were getting the best of me. One day I tried to explain my feelings to him and that I had to get away from him. I don't know whether he understood where I was coming from, but after dropping him off at home that day, I told him goodbye.

My intention was not to see him again and I drove away. I didn't call him the next day or the day after. In fact, I did not call him again. However, a few days later he called me and wanted to know what was happening. Again I tried to explain to him my feelings, to no avail. Eventually I went back, picked him up and we resumed our friendship. We became close friends and there was no sex involved. I find that when I'm not around him I worry about him. When I call him and I ask him, "Do you miss me?" He will say "yes". And I will say, "Yes, I miss you, too." Then I will tell him that I love him and he will say, "I love you, too". And so from then on, each time he calls me or I call him, we say, "I miss you and I love you".

Aphram introduced me to Ethiopian Cuisine. At first it did not appeal to me. I tried the lamb. It was chopped up in small pieces and mixed with onions, peppers and other spices. It was put over Ethiopian bread that looked like honeycomb. We would take the bread and break a small piece off, pick up the meat with the bread, using our fingers. There are only three Ethiopian Restaurants that we know of in the city limits of San Diego and we have eaten at all three. Our most favorite one is The Red Sea. I found out that Ethiopian people are very friendly and extremely inquisitive. One time I noticed at one restaurant, Aphram ordered something different than I, and when his meal arrived I was shocked to see that all his meat was uncooked. He offered to let me taste it, but I couldn't. I told him I could not eat raw meat because of my health. I had never eaten raw meat in my life and I did not like the way it looked.

Aphram told me he had a girlfriend back in Ethiopia who writes to him once in a while and recently sent him a picture. He said he has had sex a couple of times with Ethiopian women since his arrival in America.

He was a breath of fresh air that seemed to come into my life at the right moment. Early in 2004, I was suffering from depression and anxiety due to my ending my relationship with William Brown, who had left and returned to the East Coast. My relationship with Eddie Cong was another problem; he was always getting into trouble and ending up back in prison. This was combined by the death of my Uncle John, having to deal with the loneliness of living alone and not having anyone with whom to talk.

Just before I met Aphram, I had started going to a cafe called Marie's in North Park. I was aimlessly walking down University Ave by 30' Street one day and I walked into this little "mom and pop" cafe. I sat down at the counter and had a cup of coffee. While I was there I met the owner, her name, not surprisingly, was Marie. We started a conversation and she began to tell me that she had been diagnosed with breast cancer. At this time, she didn't know how serious it was and that they were still running tests. She had another doctor's appointment coming up soon concerning the seriousness of her condition. Several days later I came back to the restaurant. She told me she had learned the lump was malignant and that they were going to operate and remove both her breasts. I felt so sorry for her! I could feel the pain that showed in her eyes. That particular day she was working at the restaurant almost completely by herself except the cook, whose name was Dimitri. There were several customers there and she was very busy. I could see that she was going through a lot of pain, so I got up and helped her.

Ever since that day, I have been regularly helping her at the restaurant. And since being there, I have met some interesting people who became very good friends. One in particular we call Birdie. She's 83 years old, alert and very outgoing. She always has a smile on her face. Her favorite meal is a cheese omelet with an English muffin. She likes regular coffee with cream and no sugar. Then there's Donna, very talkative and interesting and always seems to monopolize the conversation. I find myself uplifted and enlightened every time I talk to her. One of the most unforgettable things about her is that she always orders a large bowl of grits with her meal. She can never finish them so she shares them with me. Every time she comes into the restaurant, I can expect to have grits. But thank God she only comes in once or twice a week on Saturday and Sunday! Then, there's Dennis, Ed, Duane, Josephine and Kathleen. All are very interesting people.

And there are also the waiters and waitresses. Marie has two sons, Erik and Ross, who also work in the restaurant. Erik waits tables and Ross's job is mainly to wash dishes. Then there is the cook, Dimitri, who has two sons who come in to the restaurant with their mother about once a week. Dimitri came from Mexico and everybody always compliments him on his cooking. There is Jennifer who is now in Seattle, Washington. There was Lorena. I didn't particularly like her. She was a young Spanish waitress who was very uppity and thought she knew every thing. I simply avoided her. I guess she thought Marie was allowing me to have the run of the restaurant and she resented it. She is no longer working there. She went to Atlanta to live with her brother. Rudy is a childhood friend of Erik and Ross, and Marie treats him like part of the family. His father owns the Antique Row Cafe on 30th and Adams Avenue. He has a lot of knowledge of the restaurant business because he used to work in his father's cafe. He and Erik seem to always have a personality clash. They always get into an argument about something. Then there are the new waitresses, Lulu and Amber. I think Lulu is a lesbian. I have never asked her but she has made some statements that drew me to that conclusion. She is a very friendly, outgoing and generally, a happy-go-lucky person. And finally, there is the new dishwasher, Louie, who is the nephew of Dimitri.

2004 was a very difficult year for me. Things were not going well in my personal life and I found myself very lonely. I had distanced myself from my brothers, friends and relatives. I just wanted to be alone to try to pick up the pieces of my life, which seemed to have gotten the best of me. My friend, Eddie, was still in jail and I was having some trouble keeping good help with my landscaping business. I was also coping with my depression at the same time. My social worker, Mary, would be of some help when she came for my visit every Tuesday, but in the interval, I had some severe moments of depression and I would sometimes entertain thoughts of suicide. I kept pushing and motivating myself by reading and going to the park, and getting some exercise. I knew eventually that I would have to find a more positive outlet to for my mind.

I became involved with the North Park Planning Committee and spent some time volunteering with APICAP. My involvement with APICAP and the North Park Planning Committee, along with the many friends that I had met at Marie's Cafe, seemed to help me conquer most of my fears and depression and I was beginning to feel better about myself. I truly believe that if I had not gone into Marie's Cafe that day, I would have ended up committing suicide or being committed to a psychiatric ward. My public demeanor was deceiving because underneath the facade of smiles and appearing to be a good natured person, as I presented myself to be, was a very disturbed person; a raging storm of disenchantment, disillusionment, hate and with a contempt for society. I am still struggling with the demons inside of me, but I refuse to allow them to conquer my soul and have the last laugh!

Looking back over my life I can't help but think that if life had not been so cruel to me, I could have been anything I wanted to be; a lawyer, a doctor, a mayor, a governor or perhaps even President. From the very beginning of my awareness of life, I can remember I was a sweet and loving kid. I did not just love people; I also loved the animals that surrounded me. But, the early stages of my life did not produce any positive role models. I seemed to be forever seeking someone to look up to. Being rejected by my mother and not knowing who my father was, it seemed that I was always looking for a father figure in other men. As I became older I became wiser about the world that I lived in. Even though I suffered a great deal of injustice, criticism and had been ostracized by members of my own family, I knew that there was something inside of me that wanted to give to and help others.

Some of the people in my life that I most admired were John F. Kennedy, Mother Teresa and Princess Diana. They were people who gave me the greatest inspiration in my efforts to help those who were less fortunate than myself. I kept myself motivated by continuing to reach out to those who were in need, and tried to bring some peace to those who were suffering. When I worked for Being Alive, I would go to the hospitals and homes of some of our clients on my own time to comfort them. I would take them flowers and I would sit with them and keep them company. I guess most people don't realize nor do they care, that there are a lot of people in this world who live alone or who are hospitalized with no one who care for them. These were the people to whom I was reaching out. Some of the other people in my life whom I admired are movie stars such as Bette Davis, Joan Crawford and Kathryn Hepburn. Tom Hanks and Denzel Washington, to me, are perhaps the two greatest actors. I also admired Golda Mier, Anwar Sadat, President Carter and Bill Clinton. Somehow we seem to believe that these people whom I have mentioned are bigger than life, but they are just people like you and me.

My political involvement has been significant in a way that has broadened my perspective on life. I have worked on numerous political campaigns in San Diego. I worked as a campaigner for Maureen O'Connor when she ran for mayor the first time against Roger Hedgecock. She lost by a small margin. Later on, Hedgecock was forced to resign after it was discovered that he had possibly violated campaign contribution laws. A new election was called for and Maureen O'Connor ran again for a second time. I went back to work for her in her campaign, ran her phone bank and called voters to vote for her. This time she won.

I worked in the campaigns for Ron Roberts and Bonnie Dumannis, the present District Attorney. I have often thought about running for Mayor of San Diego myself. I know I would not have won, but it was the thought of running that gave me a certain amount of pleasure. From my own perspective, I think most politicians are not only liars but are corrupt. Do I have faith in the American Justice system? The answer is no! There is no way that twelve independent, supposedly unbiased; people can render a just verdict no matter what the crime. Guilt or innocence are determined not by the wisdom and knowledge of twelve people but by the opposing attorney, and in most instances the attorney who has the most resources behind him. Simply put, it is a matter of which attorney is better equipped with the knowledge and experience of law and the amount of money the client has who will win the case.

My disdain for the judicial system goes back to my early years in Wiggins, Mississippi. My first contact with the law was when I was arrested for immoral conduct with a young boy. This was another example of blatant injustice of the system. Only because the boy was white and I black, and that our relationship was mutual, that we happened to be caught in a compromising position, was what led to my arrest and incarceration in a reformatory school. From that day on I have never trusted the law. Throughout my life I have lived in constant fear of having to defend myself against police brutality. My soul will not rest in peace until I have been totally exonerated from these miscarriages of justice that have been inflicted upon me. I have no doubt that I will one day be vindicated and the whole world will know of my innocence and how I have suffered all these years in shame.

After studying law for three years, I have come to the conclusion that our judicial system and jurisprudence is flawed in many ways. The symbol of a statue with a blindfold, which is supposed to symbolize justice that is blind; and that there is no bias regarding a person, race, religion, sexual preference or political belief comes to mind. It is far from the truth of the matter. Blind justice as it is symbolized cannot determine the truth of a crime nor can twelve individuals be impartial and without human frailties. They cannot lend eyes to a blind and outdated judicial system. We must re-analyze and revamp the system whereas it will be more consistent with freedom, justice and equality.

For the past thirty years, V.J. Ninteman and his family has kept in close contact with me. My employment with Ninteman Construction Company has provided me with a lifelong friendship with the Ninteman family, especially VJ's wife, Margaret. VJ Ninteman and Margaret had been married for 68 wonderful years until her death in 2004. Margaret was a beautiful, sweet and wonderful friend. We would go out to dinner as well as to other events together. She was a loving wife and mother. The Ninteman's had three children; two daughters, Cherie and Margaret Mary and a son, Huey. There was a host of grandchildren and great-grandchildren. When I was sent to prison for assault with a deadly weapon against Robert, I was working for VJ at the time. He and Margaret kept in close contact with me and would send me money and food packages while I was there.

After Margaret died, I visited VJ more often. Having dinner with him or just sitting in his office talking about old times. We would compose political letters to Democratic leaders with our collective views, opinions and solutions to the recent plight of the Democratic Party. Each time I visit VJ, I am fascinated as to how fluent and alert his mind is in his mid-90s, and how he would smile when we discussed past events. Once a month we go to the cemetery and place flowers on Margaret's gravesite. In 2004, VJ was involved in a car accident in which he was driving, so when we went anywhere I would drive him. I can also remember coming up the steps of his house into the living room when Margaret was alive and seeing her face, bright with a smile, as she announced, "David is here"! She was always happy to see me.

When I attended her funeral, I was seated in the front row with the rest of the family. The church was filled to capacity with family members and friends. It was a wonderful service and I think we were all pleased that Margaret was finally at peace and now in heaven. It is also a joy to visit VJ at his home when some of his grandchildren or great-grandchildren are there. His home on Marseilles Street in Ocean Beach had a wonderful view of the Pacific Ocean. From the living room window, one could watch the beautiful sun setting in the Western sky. I am certain I will never be able to repay VJ for all he has done for me; the support he has given, and the love the family has all shown me. It will be a priceless gift forever.

My contribution to the City of San Diego ranged from the building of the Coronado Bridge as a laborer working for EJ Young's Construction Company to the building of University Town Center as a carpenter helper for Ernest W. Hahn Construction Co. Also, I worked on the restoration of the Fine Arts Gallery and the Aerospace Museum in Balboa Park as a project supervisor for VJ Ninteman Construction Company. I also helped restore the historic fountain at Horton Plaza. The fountain was a very interesting job because VJ Ninteman and I had to take stairs down underneath the fountain in order to restore the foundation and the plumbing from which the water flowed. The fountain still remains a unique figure at Horton Plaza in downtown San Diego. I am very proud of the work I have done to help develop San Diego. When I first went there in 1956, San Diego was a small Navy town. Over the years I have seen it grow and expand into the grand city it is today. Even though I might have had some bad experiences in San Diego, I still love the city and call it my home.

I met Pat Washington, who holds a PhD in Women's Studies and was a professor at San Diego State University, one day at APICAP, where I learned she was a member of the board of trustees. She is a very gregarious person with a wonderful outgoing personality. She is an avowed lesbian and she was having problems getting tenure at San Diego State, perhaps because of her lifestyle. She asked me if I would help support her cause. There was a pending lawsuit against the university seeking to overturn the decision of the San Diego State Faculty Committee, which was denying her, her tenure. That day there were many people there including Toni Atkins, City Councilwoman, Nicole Ramirez, a very influential member of the gay community in San Diego and other community leaders who were supporting Pat.

I invited Pat to my 61st birthday party in December 2002, and she came. My guests included Jess San Roque, Maria Galletta, Al Bisarra, Aunt Bette and Uncle John, my brother Glen and his wife, Lisa and several other guests. We had a wonderful time celebrating my birthday.

Pat Washington is still fighting to be accepted as a professor at San Diego State University. She was recently installed as President of the San Diego Chapter of the NOW organization. She also served on several other boards and committees as a member. She continues to seek my advice on different issues and ideas, and has invited me to different workshops and events that she organizes. I consider her a very loving and caring person who always seems to be there for those who need help.

Dennis Haster, the Speaker of the House invited Marie Nealson (the owner of Marie's Cafe) to the 2005 Presidential Dinner. While there she would receive a limited edition Presidential photo. She was very excited when she received the invitation and came to me to discuss whether she should attend or not. I told her, "Of course, you MUST attend and if you decide not to, I will go in your place as Princess Charmaine!" She was invited because she is a Republican and long time member of the business community in San Diego, and for her contribution to the Republican Party. We don't know if she will go because she can't leave her business - she loves that business like a mad dog!

In the last five years I have been more forgiving toward those who have wreaked havoc on my life. This includes my feelings against the American judicial system, which has committed two gross miscarriages of justice against me. I have forgiven Puppet; the young man who helped those corrupt detectives set up and entrap me, causing my unlawful conviction of the sale of marijuana. I have forgiven the young boy, Steve, for making false statements against me because I now know it wasn't his fault, but the evil and malice work of two corrupt detectives. The miscarriages of justice have become, for me, a source of hate, frustration and animosity against all law enforcement officers. I live in constant fear of what I might do to avenge the terrible injustice that was committed against me.

In analyzing my life many times, over and over, gaining the experience in human nature and behavior as I have, my advice to mothers is that before they bring a man into their homes around their children, for any reason, they must know the individual beyond a reasonable doubt and to make sure he is not a man who will harm or molest their children! The heart sometimes misleads us but the soul of a person, to me, is never wrong. So I say to all mothers, don't follow your heart; follow your soul and God will take care of the rest!

I have been living in North Park and the same apartment for the last thirteen years. I no longer go out to bars, nightclubs, bathhouses or card rooms. I spend most of my time at home, writing, drawing, reading or watching television. The last time I smoked a cigarette or had a drink of alcohol was in the early eighties. The last time I was incarcerated was also in the eighties. For the last twenty plus years I have stayed clear of situations that would place me in jeopardy with the law. I refrain from helping young men and steer clear of any contact with law enforcement unless necessary. I dedicated most of the eighties and nineties working as a volunteer for the San Diego AIDS Foundation, Being Alive, and APICAP (Asian Pacific Islander Community AIDS Project). I found great pleasure and satisfaction in helping others especially those suffering and dying of AIDS. I received several awards and commendations for my volunteer services. This was not enough to silence the ghosts of my past or eradicate the guilt, hurt, and pains I have been subjected to by the injustice of not only a legal system that I believe in but by love ones and individuals who preyed upon my femininity and youth.

At age 64, I find myself sitting for long periods listening to the loneliness around me. Sometimes I can actually hear a voice from the past calling my name, "Charmagne, Princess Charmagne"! only to realize that I have dozed off to sleep for a few seconds. I awake and I look at each picture hanging on the wall or sitting on a table in my living room and the memories of my past began to dance before me like sugar plums in a mid-summer dream. Lady Sabrina sitting on a glass end table in a wooden mahogany frame in the living room. She has been sitting there for several years, Sabrina and I ran the streets together for years we had been close friends up until about five years ago, we drifted apart. We no longer keep in contact with each other but

I do see her once in a while. As far as I know she still lives with my brother and works as his housekeeper.

The picture of Robert in his three-piece corduroy suit hangs on the wall above the stereo set with his million-dollar smile. He was the only young man whom I truly love and still love. We spent two and a half years together and were very happy until the last several months of our relationship, which culminated in my attempt to kill him. He is now serving life in prison under the three strikes law. We are still friends and I correspond with him once in a while.

My favorite picture is of a young man with a large Afro, large brown eyes set into an olive brown face. He was a handsome and remarkable individual. It is Jimmy Rutherford, the youngest brother of Robert and the most gifted and compassionate of the three brothers. He understood and accepted the relationship between his oldest brother and I at the tender age of thirteen, he was more mature than most teens his age and became my best friend and advocate. In essence he was my son, the son I never had and because he was Robert's brother I adored him. He was the best-dressed kid at his school. I showered him with gifts and affection and gave him the security that he never had. He was killed months after I was released from prison for trying to kill his brother, Robert, in Colina Park by a gang bullet and died in Paradise Valley Hospital. He had just celebrated his eighteenth birthday. Rest well my friend, my son and I love you as always.

There is a photo of Demetric hanging on the wall in a gold exquisite European frame wearing a crystal white shirt with a dark designer tie. He was handsome, astute and intelligent. He is the apple of my eyes, my favorite nephew, the older of two boys by my younger brother, Glen Green and Regina Smith. If I had a son I would have wanted him to be like Demetric. When he was in his early teens he would visit me often against the will of his mother, father and the rest of his family. Against such pressure he would come to my place of residence and spend days with me. It took me while to get to know and communicate with him because I knew in my mind what he was going through. The accusations, lies and knowing about my sexual activities did not deter him for associating and being with me. Somehow, he knew that I love him and cared for him as a father to a son and knew that I would never harm him. While other members of the family including his parents never seemed to care for him and his brother Glen, especially his parents who was strung out on drugs, he sought the security and comfort from the only person whom has shown him love, his uncle David.

Through listening to me and adhering to my advice, he grew up to be articulate, intelligent and has a successful future ahead of him. With my assistance and a football scholarship he attended Michigan State University where he met and recently married his wife, Kimberlee. They are at the present planning for their first child and my grandchild.

I wish him and Kimberlee the best in all their endeavors.

Gen Jr., whom we call "June, June" doesn't hang in a gold frame on my wall. He is in a silver, small frame located on a shelf above the television. He is the youngest brother of Demetric. He is handsome, intriguing and self-centered. He is an introvert, difficult to reach or to understand. These qualities and traits were remarkable during the early years of this life. Now in his late twenties he has matured far more than I could have ever imagined. He still has a lot more to learn about life. Unlike his brother, Demetric, he didn't grow up under my influence nor did he share his teenage years with me. It took him some time to come to terms with my lifestyle and to accept the fact that his uncle is an avowed homosexual. Today we share a lot in common. He stays with me, he has a job. He has a young lady he is very interested in and he is expecting a child by another girl. He has promised me that he is going to support this child and be an active father. Above all he appears to listen to my advice. I have great hope for this young man and if God is willing I will have the opportunity to see him successful in whatever path he chooses.

The most unforgettable picture hanging on my wall is my beloved brother Clyde, the fourth brother of seven. A Vietnam veteran, and a high school drop out. It's the portrait of a handsome, intimidating, fascinating and somewhat unpredictable man. Sam is the oldest, and I am the second, and Sly is third. Clyde has always been a ladies man yet he was deeply troubled about his sexuality. We was very close, closer than most brothers, yet there was a love, hate relationship between us. He would confide in me when he needed some advice or had personal or legal problem. There appeared to be an intimacy between us that was not normal between brothers. There was an incident where I would come by my mom's house with a male friend of mine and he would be present. He would show resentment against my friend and exhibit antisocial behavior during the course of my visit. If the male friend were white he would react in a violent way and go as far as having a physical confrontation with my friend.

So many times he would go to gay bars with me and guys of all races would come up to him and make propositions to him. I was usually left alone while he left with one of the fellows. When I was informed that he was discovered dead in my mother's home from poison, I again was in a daze and I shed many tears. The funeral was sad. Many relatives and friends were there and I among all was the saddest. No one ever knew the intimacy we shared and I truly hope those who will know now will understand the true nature of our relationship, and the psychological reason that drives an individual to an act of love that is contrary to God's will. To this day I constantly seek divine forgiveness from God and may my brother's soul rest in peace. January 8, 1953 -- June 14, 2002.

Lady Sabrina was my best friend. We traveled the same circuit, Fifth & Market, the San Diego Red Light District, turning tricks, clipping swabbies and jarheads. Some of our dates were businessman and other permanent members of the community. Sabrina is Spanish, Black and American Indian. Beautiful, five foot ten inches tall with a deep complexion, long dark lashes and had an hourglass figure. There was no rival between us doing those early days of our friendship. It was well known among the pimps and players that I made more money in one night than any three real whores together so there was no reason for me to be jealous of Lady Sabrina because of her beauty.

We lived in the same building on 16th and L Streets, on the second floor. We had parties three to four times a week, and invited sailors, marines, gay boys, drag queens, dykes, lesbians, pimps and players. They came looking for a good time, to relieve their pent up passions and fulfilled their wildest fantasies. Lady Sabrina was my closest and dearest friend. She was present at most of my parties and those attending would be captivated by her charm and beauty. In the last several years our friendship has been estranged and once in a while I would run into him in the Hillcrest area and briefly trade a few words with him. He lives with my oldest brother Sam in the Clairemont area and since my brother and I don't get along and doesn't communicate with each other the opportunities to see him is nil. His pictures remain for years sitting on a glass end table in my living room.

My most memorable memory is the night I ran into three young, well dressed Chinese men, driving a luxury sedan on Fifth Avenue. They pulled to the curb along side of me as I strolled north to Broadway. I was dressed in a black silk cocktail dress that fell slightly above my knees with gold mesh stockings. Crowning my head was a blond wig with silver highlights that accentuated my long false eye lashes, bronze makeup, and passion pink lipstick. Draped around my neck was a gold Egyptian choker and, on my right ear a single gold loop earring dangled in the mist of a summer night breeze. Dressed to kill I was ready for anything, and there before were three of the most handsome Chinese men I have ever seen. I approached passenger side the car and one of the young men asked me if I wanted to party. YES! I replied; and got into the backseat of the car. Usually I would not get into car with more than one person, but this time I made an exception.

They took me to the Holiday Inn on First Avenue overlooking the 1-5 Freeway. We took the elevator to the 10th floor. As I walked into the room I noticed a silver gray suitcase lying in the middle of the bed opened. It was filled with bills, lots of them. One of the guys noticed me looking at the suitcase and told me that in the suitcase was $350,000 in small bills. He continued to explain that he and his partner were international hit men and that I didn't have to be afraid because they were not going to harm me. One of them removed what appeared to be a .38 magnum from underneath his coat and laid it on the bed beside the suitcase. I took a seat in a corner of the room. I watched as one of them went into the bathroom and the other two said they were going downstairs to the bar to get drinks. I was left alone with all this money before me and many thoughts ran through my mind. Especially the thought of taking the money and the gun and split. But I realized that these were indeed dangerous, professional killers for hire and I would be a fool to try second guess them, so I remained seated until the guy came out of the bathroom.

In the meantime before the other guys came back to the room whether to tell them the truth, that I was not a woman but a man, and see what their reactions were. I came to the conclusion that this would be the safest way to deal with the immediate situation, so I told him just before the other two arrived. He did not seem to be surprised but stated, "that it is hard to believe that you are a man". When the other two guys came back he told them and they seem to be somewhat surprised but smiled and said "you had us fooled". We thought you were the sexiest black woman they seen. They asked me if I knew a young black lady who would be willing to party with them. I said yes. They took me back downtown and I went into the Zebra Club and saw Tina who happened to be half black and Asian. I told her the deal and how much money was involved and she agreed. Before they left one of the Chinese guys gave me a roll of bills and I went back into the club and counted the money. It came to two hundred dollars. I was elated because I had made more money in one hour than most prostitutes make in one night. I still vividly remember all that money in the silver gray suitcase and wonder whether I made the right decision. The fact that I am still alive is proof that I made the right decision.

The most unforgettable memory of my life is when I was told that John F. Kennedy had been assassinated. I had been out all night whoring and I came home late the morning of November and was still in bed when I heard the loud bang on the door to my apartment. I got up and went to the door and when I opened it, it was Miss Noram, my next-door neighbor, was standing there with tears streaming down his face. He said, without any hesitation, John Kennedy, the president has been assassinated. I stepped back from the door, shocked, Norman came into the door and went to the living room and turned on the television. There it was, the news about the president. I saw the black limousine speeding down the road and Jackie in her pink pillbox hat leaning over the dying President. Pursued by secret service cars you could see people distraught, crying, hugging one another in despair. I felt the tears swelling in my eyes as I watched the news reports out of Dallas. Somehow it seems that my world had ended and all my dreams of the future had been erased. I could not fathom that living in America, the land of the free, that such a tragedy of this magnitude can happen. Camelot was dead. How could I go on living? How could I have faith in living knowing that evil men can kill honorable men like John Kennedy and Martin Luther King? Hate has taken over their deranged minds. Several days later I tried to commit suicide for the first time.

CHAPTER FOURTEEN

My life has been a long journey filled with rejections, loneliness and dreams deferred. I lived through World War II, the assassination of President John F. Kennedy, the resignation of President Richard M. Nixon, the impeachment of President William Jefferson Clinton and the tragedy of September 11, 2001. Love from the very beginning was a forbidden fruit laced with tears and unhappiness. Even my mother rejected me. A mother's love is important to a child and when that love is denied it has a devastating effect on the psychological behavior of the child and will remain a part of his or her life forever. The withholding of this natural emotional feeling has caused me many disappointing relationships and led to several suicide attempts and an attempted murder conviction by trying to kill Robert, my first true love. My pursuit of love and happiness has evaded me all my life and when I have seen others in love, having loving families, I have felt a deep sense of loneliness and unhappiness. Suicidal thoughts would penetrate my inner soul and life would become meaningless to me.

Loneliness has been a constant companion of mine since I can remember. As a child born with polio and shackled with a steel brace on my left leg, other kids would make fun of me and call me mean names. I felt rejected, along with no one to play with and no one who cares for me. My brothers didn't want to be around me because of my handicap and would remain at a distance from me. My mother was not at home most of the time and I never knew my father. My stepfather was molesting me and I didn't trust him. Feeling dejected and worthless pushed me farther from reality and into a world filled with fantasy. I created imaginary friends. I talked to redheaded woodpeckers, yellow-breasted hummingbirds and the forever singing blue jays. Snakes also became a part of this imaginary world: the beautiful red, yellow and black banded coral snake, the flat headed water moccasin, the sky blue roadrunners, the tan color coach whip, the gray diamondback rattlesnake, the lime green flying snakes and the graceful king snakes. Their elegant movements were fascinating. They inspired me and helped to ease the loneliness inside of me. They were not cruel, hateful or vindictive but kind, understanding and accepting. This world of make believe and God's little creatures became my hopes and dreams and I became their constant companion.

As a kid, I dreamed of becoming a great artist, a Michelangelo, Picasso or Rembrandt; a famous and renowned criminal attorney like Clarence Darrow. My fascination with art and law was far ahead of my time and I truly believe that if I had been given the opportunity, I could have been anything I wanted to be. Perhaps a noted philosopher. As I sit here today in 2007, reminiscing about my past, I can feel the pains, the anger and disappointment of dreams deferred. The memories of those fleeting moments of molestations, rapes and isolation bring bitter tears to my eyes. I can taste the hate creeping into my soul and I want to die.

Recently, walking in downtown San Diego, I walked past the Coast Hotel on Seventh and Island Avenues. I paused for a minute, remembering the day in the early Nineteen-Sixties, when I was shot, at close range, six times, by my sailor boyfriend, and fled up Seventh Avenue to Market Street, in the nude, where the police stopped me. How close I came to losing my life.

Just three blocks away, on Fifth Avenue and Market Street, on the northeast corner, is where the twenty-four-hour coffee shop, Ferris and Ferris was located. Now it is an upscale furniture and gift store. I stood on the south side of Market Street, reflecting on the many nights I spent there drinking coffee until the wee hours in the morning, chatting with other drag queens and prostitutes.

Up the street, on Fifth Avenue, near Broadway, was the Pixie 24-hour coffee shop, now a clothing store. I remember an unforgettable night, standing in the doorway of the coffee shop, talking to a young sailor friend of mine, when a cop came by, saw me and stopped. As he approached, the sailor took off. The cop asked me why I was talking to the sailor and I asked him if I was under arrest? He said no and I told him that whatever we were talking about was no business of his. As I turned around to walk back to my seat, the pulled wig off my head and a vicious fight broke out. I was arrested, taken to jail and charged with resisting arrest and assault. Later, the judge threw out the charges for insufficient reasons for the arrest.

As I continued my journey through the Gaslamp Quarter, I passed what used to be the Crossroad night club, the Zebra Club, the Kiddio #1 and Kiddio #2 Club, the Jolly Inn and Bradley's night club on Third Avenue across from Horton Plaza—all from the 1960s. Bradley's was the most famous and popular, gay nightclub at that time.

In the early 1960s, I would sit for hours in the coffee shop next Bradley's picking up dates and turning tricks because I was too young to go into the nightclubs.

Walking back to my car, to head back to my home in North Park, I marveled at the vast changes in the Gaslamp Quarter, once known as the "Red Light District" of San Diego. None of the places exist any more except the Coast Hotel, where I almost lost my life.

Looking back on my life as a young drag queen between 1959 and 1960 and a full-fledged prostitute between 1960 and 1964, I cannot believe that I survived all the evils, hate and police brutality that came with my notorious lifestyle. I still have not forgiven the corrupt detectives who were responsible for the first two convictions, 1964 and 1968, resulting in my incarceration. Sometimes I have nightmares about these detectives and, to this day, I still harbor bad feelings for those San Diego police officers as well as the Police Department as a whole. I promise myself that I will not die until I have exonerated myself from those two miscarriages of justice. One day the world will know of my innocence; my name will be restored and my soul shall be free.

Today, my life mainly revolves around my adopted son, Aphram, and my best friend, K.C. Each has a unique personality.

Aphram, an Ethiopian, speaks only limited English. He is a brilliant young man but suffered torture and abuse while held in a refugee camp in Kenya which resulted in acute depression which continues to this day. He began to hear voices and was later diagnosed with bipolar disorder. When I met him, he had been in and out of the County Mental Health system several times. After unofficially adopting him and helping him through a final, successful trip through the County Mental Health system, he is now living a normal life, sharing a two-bedroom apartment with his sister. He spends a great deal of time with me and I keep him busy, focused, motivated and compliant with his psychotropic drug regimen in a safe and positive environment, all of which keep the voices and suicidal thoughts from returning.

K.C. is from Uganda. He is intelligent and outspoken but very insecure. His insecurity is brought on by his alcohol addiction. When he drinks and becomes intoxicated, he becomes loud, moody and paranoid but never violent. When he is not intoxicated, he is pleasant, easy going and his insecurity is less apparent. He works with electronics and, when he is not drinking, he is constantly on the computer. Our relationship is based on friendship and trust. When he was homeless, I gave him a helping hand. He is now employed and coping adequately with his addiction. He is a remarkable young man and I believe he will, one day, come to terms with and beat his alcoholism.

These days, I spend a lot of time watching television, especially CNN, Fox and MSNBC news. It is my opinion that the war in Iraq was, and still is, a total disaster. We never should have been there in the first place. George W. Bush is a gun slinging cowboy, not a president. Dick Cheney is a money grabbing, secondhand vice-president. I think they both should be impeached. I have not decided whom I will vote for in the 2008 Presidential Election. I am leaning toward Hillary Clinton. I believe that Barrack Obama has the potential but not the experience or the political wherewithal to cope with the crooks in Washington.

Hate has taken center stage in the lives of people all over the world and their fear of each other has continued to feed the fire of racism and religious conflicts. Global warming, political strife and racism are just a few problems that future generations will have to deal with and find viable solutions. I can take solace in the fact that I will not be around to witness the turmoil of these events.

I keep asking myself, "How could a young, gifted, black boy with large hazel eyes and a loving heart go from the southern heart of Mississippi to a homeless 16-year-old in Southern California, becoming a drag queen, a whore, a prostitute before the age of twenty-one?" It is hard to believe that I am still alive at the age of sixty-five, after having been sexually assaulted, raped numerous times, shot once, stabbed once, after several suicide attempts and sixteen years of cruel and brutal imprisonment. The scars of all those painful years are still visible in my mind. I truly hope that no one else has to walk in my footsteps.

2003

In 2003, I became very depressed and suicidal. I consulted with my case manager about my problem and she suggested that I should have a therapist. She arranged to have a therapist from the County come by once a week and assist me with my depression. The first time I met Mary, my therapist, I was impressed with her professionalism, elegance and charm. She was an imposing woman with beautiful blue eyes, light auburn hair and a charming smile that set my heart at ease and left no doubt that I could trust her in helping me to overcome my fears. The first session was enlightening, stimulating and motivating. She immediately took control by setting the mood of the conversation. "Would you like to tell me a little about yourself?" she asked. As I began to elaborate on my past, she was attentive and focused on every word. When I finished, she said, "You have had a very interesting life, and what an amazing journey it has been for you." The first session was indeed a success. I felt more relaxed and much more in tune with reality.

One day, while we were discussing recent world issues, she asked me if I ever thought about writing the story of my life. "Yes," I said. I told her that I had compiled hundreds of notes and documentation about my past life and had been thinking about putting it all together. She told me she had a friend, who lived on the east coast, who loved to write and probably would assist me in writing my life story. Her friend would be coming out to California for a vacation in a few months and she would ask her about helping me. I was delighted and would be looking forward to seeing her.

A couple months later, Mary called me and informed me that her friend was in town and that she would bring her over on her next visit with me. The day I met Becky, in 2004, I knew I had found someone who would give me the will power, determination and motivation to fulfill my dream of completing my autobiography.

Becky came to my apartment with her laptop at least twice a week for several weeks. She would type on her keyboard as I told her the story of my life. Every now and then, she would stop and ask me to explain in more detail about a certain person I had mentioned or elaborate more about an incident that had happened to me. She would push me, goad me and lead me for hours until I couldn't go any more. Finally, I would give in and tell her that it was enough for that day. I was amazed how much we accomplished in the few weeks we had to work with.

Before she left for the east coast, Aphram and I accompanied her to Borrego Springs. Aphram and I had never been to Borrego Springs but Becky had been there before. We all went in my car. The drive to Borrego Springs was beautiful. It was in the beginning of summer. The flowers along the road were in bloom, the trees were turning different colors and the sun was bathing the countryside with its violet rays. I was elated to be going somewhere out of the City with friends to relax and have fun. Becky told us about the beautiful, exotic plants, flowers and the unique species of cactus growing in and around Borrego Springs. We had our cameras and snack sacks and my heart was filled with excitement. We arrived in the early afternoon. The sun was beating down directly on our heads and the temperature was in the triple digits when we checked in at the information center, got maps of the surrounding areas and looked at the exhibits on the walls of the information center.

For the next two hours, we roamed the landscape, finding exotic plants and flowers, taking pictures as we went. The flowers were gorgeous. I have never seen such beauty, in person, in all of my life and I will never forget this experience.

As we walked down the trails surrounded by all those beautiful flowers, I watched the joy that lighted up Aphram's face and I knew it was a blessing to bring him along. Such an experience will lift him up and give him more will power and determination to overcome his deep-seated depression and keep the demons away from his soul. Before we left, we stopped at a restaurant that appeared to be a relic of a southwestern diner. The menu consisted of Mexican dishes, old-fashioned hamburgers, beers, whisky and Spanish-style tequila drinks. The food was excellent and the country and western music gave it an extra taste of nostalgia.

We arrived back in San Diego late in the evening. I was totally exhausted. Aphram and I saw Becky to her car and bid her a good night. We retired for the evening, watching TV and talking about the plants and flowers we had seen.

The next day, Aphram and I went to a pottery and gift shop on Ray Street in North Park and purchased a going away gift for Becky in appreciation for all her help and the valuable time spent with us. The gift was a beautifully colored vase with a European flavor. We had it beautifully wrapped by a professional in a gift shop in Hillcrest. I called Becky the following day and asked her to stop by the apartment before she left. She came by the next day and we gave her the gift. She was surprised and elated. We said our goodbyes and she left. I have talked with Becky on the phone several times since she has been back home. I will never forget her. She was the inspiration to keep me in focus, which allowed me to finish my autobiography.

For years, I blamed everyone except myself. Indeed, there is a lot of blame to go around but I have to accept some responsibility for mistakes and hardship. I never claim to be an angel but far from being a devil. I love people regardless of race, color or differences. Within the last several years, I have shown a deep compassion for the elderly, homeless, the sick and, especially those who are suffering from HIV, AIDS and cancer. In reaching out to others, I am trying to make amends for hurt and pain I have caused others and to ensure my immortality.

I constantly question the existence of God, yet know deep in my soul there is someone bigger and superior that controls the universe and determines the destiny of all of us. Often, I pray for forgiveness and understanding and ask God to show me the way to peace for my soul. I know that he is listening for each day he brings me more joy and peace than I have ever had before and I am determined to survive until the redemption of my soul is fulfilled.

The world is moving at a breathtaking speed and I seem to be standing still like a prisoner locked into a time capsule. Computers, cell phones, DVDs, Ipods and other modern technologies have made me feel insecure and confused. I am amazed how the younger generation takes life for granted with no compassion for those less fortunate and shows no regard for the sick and elderly in society, with the rise of violent crimes sexual assault, mothers abandoning their newborns, husbands killing their wives and wives killing their husbands; the conflict in the Middle East, the genocide in Sudan and the millions of peoples suffering with HIV and AIDS all over the world. Looking back, my life wasn't so bad after all. I survived. Was it worth all the pain, disappointments and dreams deferred? That is a question I cannot answer because I had no control over my destiny. I believe that most if not all things are already determined and we play only a small role in shaping our lives.

I am truly grateful to all the people who have helped me along this way and have made a positive contribution to my unique understanding of life. For life to me is just a simple journey with no beginning or ending. The Soul of a man goes on forever; only the flesh is left behind.

Before I leave you with the story of my life, I must say to all the Moms of the world, God bless you all. Without you, there would be no life. The love of a mother is one of God's greatest gifts but the greatest gift of all is the fruit of a mother's womb, a child. It is a precious gift. Take special care and love. Moms be very careful to whom you trust your precious jewels. Don't allow your guard down because of the weakness of the flesh or the deceitful beat of the heart. There are men who will deceive you to get to your children and your precious jewels will be tarnished or forever stolen from you. To young couples who are planning on having kids, be sure you are ready and make sure you are financially and mentally able to provide for your children. I love kids but unfortunately for the sexual abuse I experienced as a child and the tragic miscarriage of justice in 1967, the fear of being around or in the presence of children has plagued me most of my life. I think I would have been a great father and a good husband but I have accepted the hand I have been dealt and make the best of my present situation.

I don't expect to live much longer. My AIDS problems are getting the best of me. Being aware of all the negativism recently and my feeling of being worthless have increased my suicide idelations and the constant reminder of deaths of friends and relatives have made its extremely hard to continue this life journey alone. There are two things that keep my sanity intact: first, my adopted son, Aphram, and my determination to finish this story and to see it is published.

While studying world history in college, I read a reference to Hannibal, the Carthaginian general. It was said, "wherever his horse had trodden, the grass would never grow again." I truly hope no kid will ever travel where my footsteps have trodden, so that his or her live will always be filled with love, beauty and happiness.

CHAPTER FIFTEEN

Now, as I sit here in the Southern California sun on my patio reading the newspaper, I pause to contemplate my future and to reflect on my past. I had to ask myself what happened to my life? Was my life destiny to be lonely, loveless and filled with heartaches, disappointments and tears? Did God forsake me? Why? Did my suffering have to do with the sins of my father? Was I cursed for being born on Christmas Day? Whatever the reasons for all the turmoil in my life, it was hell. Looking back, I see a small, frail Black kid with a heavy steel brace on his left leg and, looking deep into his hazel eyes, I see the hunger, pains and confusion that lie deep in his soul. The world around him was strange and his desire to belong and to be loved appeared to have no meaning. He alone was facing a reality that was far beyond his comprehension. He lacked the capacity to understand the nature of his existence. He knew he belonged, but where? There was no one to turn to. Father unknown, mother never at home. Each day as he moved without emotion, he wished for someone to be with, to love, to comfort him when he felt lonely and unhappy.

That little kid is still inside me, begging to be heard, to be known, still seeking the love that had been denied all these years. Over the years when someone criticized me, I would ask myself, what does he or she know about me? Do you have any knowledge what I have been through as a child? How would you like to walk in my footsteps, growing up in the Deep South in the 1940s, being used as a sex toy and discriminated against because of my handicap, and high profile sexual behavior? It is so easy for someone to criticize another person because he or she is different, without understanding what caused that person to be different.

I have lived constantly with harassment, intimidation and discrimination because of my feminine behavior, belief, and sexual proclivities. I feel strongly that people should mind their own business and leave other people to themselves. Perhaps if I had not been molested, misused and abused as a child, I could have grown up as a heterosexual with a loving family, an ambitious career, and a beautiful home overlooking the Pacific Ocean. What fate had determined for me is who I am today.

I believe that I had no control over my destiny and for me to try to change my life at this junction of my life would be fruitless, for deep inside of me I would still be the same. I am what I am at this stage of life and nothing is going to change my sexual orientation. For the last three years I have had no desire to indulge in any sexual activities. I have not been involved in a relationship since 2003 and my interest in men has faded to a distant memory.

The year 2007 has been, so far, a good year for me. The challenges of the past are long gone, only the memories remain, to keep me safe and free from the burning desire of the flesh and the emotional pains of my damaged soul. I now spend most of my time reflecting on some of the positive things I have accomplished. One of my greatest accomplishments is when, in my early 30s, I decided to get my high school diploma and go to college. I was amazed, while attending Educational Culture Center (ECC) and San Diego City College I made straight-"A"s three semesters in a row and was listed on the Dean's Honor List in my Law classes. I had high hopes and dreams but my diagnosis of HIV and the decrease in my energy and memory put an end to those hopes and dreams. Once again, I felt abandoned, alone, depressed, and God had forsaken me.

Many of my friends, associates and co-workers have died of AIDS and HIV complications, some with agonizing and excruciating pain, others less suffering, but intense pain. These painful memories have left me questioning not only the existence of God but my own existence. Sometimes I feel that I'm dreaming and the world around me is only a figment of my imagination.

I remember the many unique jobs and the inspiring and motivating people I met along the way. Working for Mercy Rehab and Convalescent Center on Fourth Avenue was rewarding, inspiring and educational. I started as a Certified Nurse Assistant (CNA) and, after a short period as a CNA, I was asked to become a Medical Records Clerk, which I graciously accepted. Being a Medical Records Clerk gave me the chance to free myself from the demanding tasks of patient care and an opportunity to the challenge of exercising my abilities on a more intellectual level. I was very successful as a Clerk and I made many friends and a few enemies. One of my favorite CNAs and a friend is Cloteal. She was an exceptional Nurse's Assistant, compassionate and extremely accurate in charting. Today, she is a patient at the same convalescent hospital, in her early 50s, with a serious illness. I have been to visit her several times. I hope and pray that whatever happens, God will take care of her and give her the compassion that she has given to thousands of others.

As Head Carpenter's Helper for Earnest W. Hahn Construction Co, building UTC in La Jolla, my duties were to make sure that all carpenters had workable equipment and ample supplies at all times and to supervise the other Carpenter's Helpers in assisting me to carry out my duties. Mr. Hunter, my Labor Foreman, was a well-trained person and one of the very few Blacks who held such a position in a major construction company in San Diego. We became good friends. I learned a lot from him and he contributed greatly to my self-esteem and inspired me to become the best that I could be. When Earnest W. Hahn built Horton Plaza, I wanted to be a part of its construction but, at the time, I was working for another company. I ran into Mr. Hunter several times, after UTC. He is still working for Mr. Hahn's construction company.

The Ninteman Construction Company was spearheaded by two brothers, Vince J. Ninteman and Lambert Ninteman. I worked for the Ninteman Construction Company from 1976 to 1978. As Supervisor of the yard, my duties were to maintain all machines and equipment, purchase supplies for the yard, main office and jobsites. After purchasing supplies for each job site, it was my obligation to see that these supplies reached whatever job sites ordered them and make sure they received them on time.

V. J. Ninteman was my boss. I took orders and reported to him only. Lambert left the company not long after I was employed. Vince had a nephew named David. He was ten years old and would come to the shop occasionally and I ended up supervising him. Right away I noticed that he was a troubled kid. It was years later before I realized the extent of his psychological problems. One day at the shop, I was busy with a project and David was there and suddenly there was a commotion and as I turned around, I saw David standing in front of an electrical cutting machine with white paint splattered all over his face, on the wall and floor. I walked over, cut off the machine and took David aside and cleaned the paint off his face and chastised him for his behavior. From that day on, I never had any problem with him again. David's life continued to spiral out of control as he grew older which lead to his imprisonment several times. During this period, most of his family members disassociated themselves from him. His father had died from alcoholism when David was in his early teens. I never wavered from supporting him and until this day I have remained his most loyal and confident supporter. He has two remarkable kids, Ashley and Justin. He was released from prison in 2006 and is in the process of operating his own company called David Ninteman's Painting and Construction Company. Notwithstanding his personal and psychological problems, he is smart, intellectual and a remarkable person. His undying love for his kids is basically the result of rejection he received from his father and from the dysfunctional problems that existed between his father and mother due to his father's alcoholism. Today, David Ninteman is coping with his problems and is making tremendous progress towards being a productive member of "our" society.

Several years ago, my brother Sam and I took a trip back to Wiggins, Mississippi to visit our birthplace. This was the first time I had been back to Mississippi since I left there in 1956. Wiggins has not changed much. It was still a small sleepy Southern town with wood frame houses sitting on small, dusty lots. We visited several homes of people we knew and the site where we grew up as kids. The white shotgun house was gone. The area where the house stood was overgrown with small trees and weeds. The property still belongs in the family and we went to the local deed office to receive some legal papers attesting to our ownership.

We visited the local cemetery located at the same church we attended as children. The spot where the outhouse stood and where Bobby Ray and I made love was still there. I stood there as the memories of those two naked bodies writhing on the dirt floor, tasting the bittersweet, forbidden fruit of life. I felt sadness, guilt and shame. As we entered into the cemetery, I seemed drawn to a particular spot and suddenly my feet stopped. I was standing over a bronze plaque and I looked down and read the inscription. It read, "Oscar Thompson." I was standing there with the name staring back at me. Sam came and stood beside me. He read the inscription and said, "Oscar Thompson. He is the one that would sneak into your bed at night. He is the one that also molested me. Isn't it ironic that we stand here to day over his grave?" Finally, I began to understand the meaning of his words. A great relief seemed to come over me as if I had been redeemed of the evil spirit that had possessed me all those years before and I had finally conquered the demons inside of me. Tears began to swell in my eyes and at last I felt vindicated. When we left the cemetery, I took a final glance at the spot of the outhouse and asked myself, why.

Now, I must bid you farewell. I have lived, yet I have not lived. I hope that my story has enlightened someone's life and others have gained enough knowledge to cope with life's problems and enable parents to raise their children with love, compassion and to protect them from the evil that exists around them. I will see you somewhere, somehow in the future and until then, farewell my friends and may God be with you always.